Angela Brock

Acknowledgment: I would like to thank God for allowing me to have the courage to step out on faith and tell my truth. My son Jyjuan also has been a big inspiration. I want to thank men and the women who have been through the same struggles, same heartaches, same fears, same insecurities, inadequacies but dared to go inside and get free from the bondage of self. My writing not only talks about pain, heartaches, struggle, disappointments, failures but also having the courage to overcome them. *If you Only Knew How God Turned My Mess Into A Message.* Some of my writings have adult language. Music gave me titles and different subjects to write about. My life hasn't been easy, and far from perfect, God is still working on me.

In my acknowledgement I would like to thank My husband who at times don't think I recognize the unconditional love he has given me and my sons all these years. It was'nt easy but he hung in there. Also I want to thank Marcus Harvey who supported me through a rough time when my Jyjuan was going through his difficulties to find himself. Also Mrs Anderson and her assistance Vicky Beatties to allow the ladies from MOMS to have each other as a support system to heal from the absence of their love ones who are incarcerated. Words alone could never express the my gratitude. EbonyDawn Starks from Writers Block Publishing LLC, who published my sons two books and mine. Thank you so much for allowing us both to have a voice.

Perhaps when you thought you were not good enough, the truth, you were overqualified. Beyonce said it best; your self-worth is determined by you; you don't have to have someone to tell you who you are. Perhaps falling in love with the one in the mirror, who has been through so much but is still standing.

If You Only Knew How God Turned My Mess Into A Message

At the beginning of my book are different inserts of my life, experiences, and hope. Allowing myself to be transparent, and in the same token, I'm healing. I overcame many doubts, so many tears, many changes, challenges, courage, a lot of pain, perseverance, and most definitely healing. I couldn't ask God enough for His Grace and Mercy even when I didn't deserve it.

Angela Brock

Table of Content

Introduction: Quick Rundown

Chapter 1: Current Situation

Chapter 2: The Past

Chapter 3: Take a look out of my window

Chapter 4: Fight is fixed

Chapter 5: Broken But Not scattered

Chapter 6: Take a Walk In My Shoes

Chapter 7: Not who I am, but whos I am

Chapter 8: Walk like your going somewhere

Chatper 9: Mirror Mirror

Chapter 10: At The end of the Road

Chapter 11: Dealing with rejection

Chapter 12: A Woman Worth

Chapter 13: Coming to terms

Chapter 14: Take Me as I am

Chapter 15: God Plan

Chapter 16 Forgive me of my sins

Chapter 17: Free yourself

If You Only Knew How God Turned My Mess Into A Message

Chapter 18: Is it sex or a relationship

Chaper 19: Connection with others

Chapter 20: Why Do I Stay Pass the Expiration Date

Chapter 21: Awakenings

Chapter 22: I'm still standing

Chapter 23: Giving Myself Permission to Take Care of Myself

Chapter 24: Amends and Reconciliation

Chapter 25: It's Necessary to Be Me Because Everyone Else is Taken

Chapter 26: My Shero

Chapter 27: Having a better perspective of my life

Chapter 28: Mr. Wrong

Chapter 29: Life is an Adventure

Chapter 30: Unresolved issues

Chapter 31: Out with the old in with the new

Chapter 32: Ageing

Chapter 33: My Shero

Chapter 34: Is it worth the investment

Chapter 35: Co-Dendency no more

Chapter 36: Self- Acceptance

Angela Brock

Chapter 37: Am I My sister keeper

Chapter 38: Lil Sis

Chapter 39: Lil Bro

Chapter 40: Sisterhood reunion of the heart

Chapter 41: Being a single mom to my two sons

Chapter 42: Dear Momma

Chapter 43: Words from the heart

Chapter 44: Family

If You Only Knew How God Turned My Mess Into A Message

Introduction

A Quick Rundown

I was born Angela Adell Brock on August 22, 1964, to high school sweethearts, my mother, Darryl C. Arnold, and father, William J. Billy Brock. My parents conceived me at the impressionable age of sixteen. By the time my mother was eighteen, she had already birthed two children, me at seventeen and my sister, Lorraine, aka Rainey, at eighteen.

As you can imagine, my sister Rainey and I grew up very close because we were only fourteen months apart and were each other's keepers. Though my parents were a young married couple, my sister and I had a fairly good childhood through grade school, growing up in the Elmore Square Projects (before this area became a war zone and later torn down) with the help of my aunt Corrine and her husband, my Uncle Newt. We were both extremely intelligent, and our grades on our report cards always reflected this fact.

By the time I was nine, in 1973, my mother had birthed her only son, my brother Darrell, who she had named after herself by another man. By this time, my mother and father had already split and divorced because of what I later learned to be my father's drug use and infidelity. Growing up, I was always searching for something to comfort the void that lived inside of me. I remember like it was yesterday; I visited different churches sometimes with friends, but most of the time alone. For as long as I can remember, I was always told I had an old soul by my aunt and uncle, who I considered more like my grandparents.

Angela Brock

My mother was a hard-working woman who always maintained a job and went to Ccac for Social Work and then attended the University of Pitt and received her bachelor in Education. Due to my mom being a single parent, I began to take on a surrogate mother's role in her absence to my brother and sister. My mom was diagnosed with lung disease, Sarcoidosis, and still maintains three jobs to support her growing family. The woman in my life was very strong, like my mom and my great aunt, who I called my grandmother, always stress the importance of education, so I proceed to make good grades. Still, my curiosity of the streets seemed attractive, as I mention in the beginning that void that continues to haunt me, and for years I seek out to fulfill it. All my choices weren't always positive, but it gave me temporary relief.

While I was in high school, before graduating, my sister and I were always very popular, beautiful, intelligent, had the latest clothes, and street smart. I enjoyed dancing. My two friends and I used to compete in talent shows and were extremely good. I attended Schenley Highschool, and I was also a Pom-Pom girl for the Schenley Spartans. During this time, I was forced into a role as the primary caretaker of my youngest siblings, and everywhere I went rather to after school events, summer jobs, my younger siblings were with me. I always continue to maintain good grades, even though being the oldest demanded a lot of responsibility. After graduating from high school, I decided to go to school for Retail Business Management. I wanted to be a Buyer, due to my creative way of dressing, I thought this would be a right career choice. I decided to go to Bradford School of Business for a year and a half. My father was sporadically in my life, and my sister and I both started frequent trips to New York City with my father and his family as teenagers and young adults. This is where I subconsciously came to escape, I guess.

If You Only Knew How God Turned My Mess Into A Message

I also first began experimenting with drugs during this time and place of my life. At that time, I thought it was all in fun, never knowing that at that moment, I would later resent the choices I made. Even though I finish the Bradford School of Business, my efforts to do something with the knowledge I learn became a second priority in my life for this; my life would forever change; again. The cousin I used to visit in New York went to the Navy and was station in Rhode Island, I went to stay with her to get my life back on track, but that was only temporary.

After high school, life was a blur of working, drugs, parties. I did not think I had a drug or emotional problems and still kept my baby and brother and sister close to my bosom through all this. At the age of twenty, on November 29, 1984, I birthed my son, Jyjuan. I went into labor early. Now I'm a single mother, and now what feels like raising three children but only biologically a mother to one. I had my place by then. I had yet to think I had a drug problem at this point. My apartment in Arlington Heights was laid out, and bills were paid. I maintained a job, went to Job Corp, and enrolled in the college program to continue my education. My son and siblings were my world, and I wanted better for my son and them.

Fast forward to five years later, my son Jaylon was born on August 28, 1989. This time, his father is around, he accepts and taken on responsibility for raising my firstborn, and he is a good provider. Only by now I had graduated to more serious drugs. My sign of addiction was beginning to show. I remember praying to God and asking him to help me; I'm talking about a heartfelt cry God answered.

Angela Brock

After years of abusing my body, getting physically abused, and doing drugs; I finally made a conscious decision to stop. I check into a 30-day rehab, and my days of using drugs and alcohol ended July 25, 1993. Before being released and trusting myself to these hard streets, I checked myself into a six month halfway house because I needed more structure and coping skills. While I was there, I start looking into what I might want to do with my new life and started again to pursue my education but continued to have obstacles in my life with my children and finding proper housing. So I join an outpatient women's recovery program with the Hill Collaborative, where I started healing. In 1999 WPIC wanted to create a community-based program in the Hill District where I was born and raise and wanted a person in their program to work with the other woman and their kids who struggle with drug abuse, emotional problems. I was chosen as a Family Support Coordinator to empower, educate, and help navigate mental health and drug abuse that affects the family.

This job took me to places I could never imagine, like New Mexico, Puerto Rico, Minneapolis, and Washington DC. I share my experience of navigating the Mental Heath agency for my children and getting paid for it. I sat at the table with judges, directors of juvenile faculties, and more. The amazing thing God did, he took me to the community I grew up. I work from 1999 to 2004 when the grant finished. This experience opens the door for me to know what I wanted to do in my life and my purpose, so I enrolled in CCAC for drug and alcohol and criminal Justice in 2009. My mom passed away, and that when I gave my life to Christ. I join Macedonia Church. I graduated in 2011 in drug and alcohol counseling but still needed a couple of math credits to complete my criminal Justice. In 2012 I started looking into schools for my bachelor's degree. One evening I had class, and I

If You Only Knew How God Turned My Mess Into A Message

had prayed to God showed me a sign. Geneva school was the only recruiter present. I retrieved my transcript and gave it to the recruiter. In 2012 my dad pass away and at that time being the I was the only person responsible for handling all his affairs so going to Geneva was push back. Throughout the years, the recruiter would call me to see if I was interested in attending Geneva College. In January 2015, I was contacted again by a different recruiter offering a grant for Community Ministry and Leadership right after one of my best friends committed suicide, and I decided to go for it.

I'm so blessed to say that I have remained cleaned through the many trials and tribulations that life has taken me through. My best friend, my sister Rainey, was brutally murder on November 13, 1996, at such a crucial time of my sobriety. I've lost both my parents and dear friends as well, and through it all, God has seen me through as I am still sober. Today, I know you have to go through many tests to have a testimony, and only my story gives me glory.

I've been blessed with clarity and no longer have to be super woman to fix others' problems but fix my own. You don't know how a weight has been lifted—being a rescuer now rescuing me. Many positive doors have opening up. I now have the courage, strength, and wisdom to walk through.

So there you have it, my life in a nutshell; If you only knew *how God turned my mess into a message.*

Angela Brock

Chapter 1: Current Situation the Present

It's 2020, the pandemic of the Corona Virus is killing thousands of people, and our country is going through a recession. People are losing their jobs, homes, and not able to provide food for their families. The pandemic stressors have had families being disconnected from their loved ones' lives, which has put everyone in a sad state of confusion, uncertainty, mentally unstable, confined, and unable to go and come freely. Living in fear, people walking around with masks and gloves to protect themselves, and those around them do not know the differences between a stick-up man or girl or a person who is just trying to protect themselves.

Living in a predominantly black community and seeing first hand the struggle, addiction is really prevalent. Addicts walking around like the living dead, with no hope, despair, confused and lost. It's sad to see. I started remembering the time that I was in total darkness, feel with pain, heartaches, fear and no hope. I felt hopeless because I had brought into the enemy lies of self-deception, but God saved me by his grace and mercy even when I did'nt think I deserved it.

It feels like we're in our last days. People are going through difficulties. 2 Timothy 3:1-27 For people will be lovers of self, lovers of many, proud, arrogant, abusive. Our children will disrespect their parents, finding yourself ungrateful, heartless, slanderous, without self-control, brutal, not loving God, treacherous, reckless, have more pleasure of others than lovers of God, and denying his power.

In this book, I explore life lessons, heartache, pain, strength, perseverance, addiction, life lessons, and confession of one's sins once you come to your truth. This book exercises life lessons, life failure, life disappointment, potential love, bad choices,

If You Only Knew How God Turned My Mess Into A Message

confession, loss of hope, pain, hurt, and trial and tribulation I went through to find myself.

Finding me was the most painful thing, but also the most joyful rewards. Thinking of all the things I have been through and how God held my hand through it all, he never left me forsaken.

Angela Brock

Chapter 2: The Past

Growing in the era in the sixties, it was a weird time. Back then, you were considered a boomer baby, and was the end of the Vietnam War; this is when the Civil Right Movement started. While most households had mom and dad, plus a boatload of kids-families in your neighborhood was unended. This was a time when your neighbor could whip your ass, and when you got home, you got another ass whipping from your parents. The moms started to wear the pants, and some of them had full-time and part-time jobs to provide for their families. In my case, there's wasn't a father role model in my household. My mom was the head of the household; my childhood wardrobe consists of chucks, pro-kids, overall jumpers that I still rock today.

In the summer, someone would turn on the fire-hydrants to cool us off from the heat. My mom had card parties and socials and sold dinners to provide for her family; this went on all weekend. I didn't know we were struggling to make ends meet; actually, I thought I was quite fortunate because we never miss a meal. My sister and I had all the latest clothing, with the absence of a father. The people who watched my sister and me had a bunch of kids; every time my mom dropped us off, we had to fight until my mom came to get us. This situation was unhealthy for any child who had to fight their way through. At the age of ten, my mom and grandmother decided they wanted more for my sister and me, and now I have a brother. We move to Sugar-Top, Milwaukee Street, into a duplex where my grandmother lived downstairs, and my mom and my siblings live upstairs.

Five years later my mother had a baby girl, my life was never the same. I went from being a teenager doing teenage stuff to stepping in a role as a mother to my siblings. My mother was

If You Only Knew How God Turned My Mess Into A Message

diagnosed with a lung disease called Sarcoidosis. Many nights my mom didn't hear my sister crying or knew when she needed her diaper to be changed, so early on, I became a caretaker for my siblings. I no longer hung-out with my peers because I needed to help my mom. The only time I had a break was when the summer approached; I spent my summers with my dad's family in New York City. New York is where I learned the game of hustling. I didn't know my dad was an addict until I indulged in experimenting with different drugs myself. Boosting became second nature for me; I stole most of my school clothes and pocket the money given to me to go to school shopping. People-pleasing came naturally because I always had money and drugs to entertain the company that I had to have around me.

As I reflected on my earlier years, like with my baby-sister, every time my mom paid her to look after my sister and me, her husband would beat her and take the money. I started looking at the same behaviors in my dad, the nodding, long sleeve shirts in the summer, his whole demeanor change in a blink of the eye.

Angela Brock

Addiction

My first sexual experience was at the age of thirteen, I got pregnant for the first time exploring sexual activities, full of fear and confused, but I knew I wasnt ready to become a mother. I was still a kid myself. Still searching for me, I meet another gentleman. I was fifteen now. He was loving and caring, and very supportive of my emotional needs. I said, is my Mr. Wrong; there's something in me that cries out for failure. I was not comfortable with the traditional healthy relationships because they seem boring; there was no excitement. I was addicted to fancy that Bonnie and Clyde shit, hustling, and the bustling in life. True to the game, but the ones I was involved with, was dull, lacking excitement but healthy. I am talking about the distorted perception of a man. I didn't have any positive male role models to show me how a man is supposed to treat you. My mother had her own addiction and it wasn't to drugs. I'm just addicted to whatever comes my way. My first time, my heart was broken by my high-school sweetheart, an accusation was made that he slept with my sister, you talking about your heart being torn out, having two people you love betrayed you.

Still searching became very promiscuous, laying up not for love but a feeling of lust, not protecting myself sexually it's only through the Grace of God I didn't catch the H.I.V.; that's real talk. Half of the men I met were in the occasion club spots I would hit up on the weekend, you talking about chasing a feeling. Today I know it was a void that only God can feel it. So now I'm in my young adult-hood, running a little too fast at time. Just a little girl in this big world is trying to find love in any man's eyes. The streets had me; I'm talking about the lifestyle, loved everything about it. Making frequent trips to New York on the regular, for supplies and demand, Now I'm caught up in the grip of addiction,

If You Only Knew How God Turned My Mess Into A Message

I'm using, but I'm talking about the lifestyle. It's a saying, "A monkey can't sell bananas." if you know what I mean. I became my best customer; this went on for years.

All my dreams and inspiration went out the door, 1993 I had enough of how I was living, Now I had two sons, one who was truly affected by my bad decision in men, and the second one, came out of the womb not giving a shit. All the abuse, all the pain, all the suffering, the drugs couldn't even suppress what I was trying to cover up. The most profound prayer I said was God help me; at that moment, for the first time, I felt a heartfelt surrender, beyond my understanding, God heard my cry. Now it's 27 years later, and I'm amazed at the woman I'm becoming; I'm not talking about material possession; I'm talking about internal peace. Being free to be me, I'm free from the bondage of my self-deception that I brought into for many years. I have a second life to live.

Angela Brock

Generational Curses

Generational curses are believed to be passed down from generation to another due to rebellion against God. Suppose your family lies with a single family household, mental health, incest, divorce, poverty, anger, promiscuous behaviors, dying with a broken heart, and other ungodly patterns. You're likely under generational curses. The Bible says that these curses are tied to choices our familiar and have the greatest influence on my development of patterns of sins.

The generational curse I'm talking about continues to happen to the women in my life, such as my grandmother, mother, siblings, children, and their children. Mental health is real. It denies the women in my generation to find their worth. I'm not talking about financial stability, career choices, where they live, where they have traveled. I'm talking about their emotional state. My mother's mother was paranoid -schizophrenia, intelligent but died with a broken heart. My mother was intelligent, an overachiever, The rock of the family, and died with a broken heart. Her behavior showed a sinful nature, like being promiscuous, which passed down to her children, never having healthy relationships with the opposite sex. It was sad, but it's true. I can remember as a young girl searching for love and acceptance through men; I visited different churches trying to fill the void that only God can. I knew early on that I was in a spritual warfare within myself. Alcoholism, drug addiction, sex addiction, co-dependency addiction, people-pleasing addiction, finding validation, and became an addict. I never knew my worth being a addicted. Because I found myself compromising and settling for less, knowing I was worthy of better, but I didn't know better, and even once I knew better, it was so ingrained from generation to generation of women that model their belief system.

If You Only Knew How God Turned My Mess Into A Message

So I ask myself what can I do to break this generation of curses? The first thing that came to my mind is to lead by example with my grandchildren and show my granddaughter their worth; they don't have to use their bodies for acceptance and love. Let them know their body is God's temple. If it's not spiritual, it's not pratical, also be a woman with integrity and respect for themselves and never rely on anyone to take care of them unless they are worthy of having them—my grandson how to treat a lady with dignity and respect and take care of there family. So I got my hands full; I can't fix the past, but I can die trying, so my grandchildren don't be affected by my generational curse with the help of God. Curses destroy families but with God, healing anything is possible.

Angela Brock

Loneliness; Enemy Within

All of us, at one point in time, dealt with loneliness within. It's something that can grip you in the blink of an eye, in a seductive way, and comes out of nowhere because there is a void or a hole in your soul that makes you feel alone. Addiction plays the same role; it doesn't have to mean using a chemical; it can be anything, like sex, shopping, eating, overworking, gambling, that include scratch-off, lottery, anything that takes you outside yourself for instant gratification. Loneliness wears many customs, sadness, depression, anxiety, being fear; all these are signs of isolation that causes loneliness.

Now I'm clean; it's a different type of loneliness because now you're coming into your truth. Being in a room full of people but still feel alone because you're not willing to minimize your intellect to be socially accepted, able to be honest about you, where folks sway away because your free to be you. Never felt connected, always rejected. Being fake has never been a part of my costume, never changing depending on the company I was around. Either I fuck with you are I didn't. I never needed a bunch of folks to violate my presence—a loner by nature, able to be in my own company. Rather be with me, it's less complicated. If there's no enemy within, the enemy outside can not harm me as I can. So be aware of no one can hurt you more than yourself. We carry our worst enemies within ourselves, and his enemies can measure a man's greatness. Be good to yourself because you can be your worse enemy.

If You Only Knew How God Turned My Mess Into A Message

Take a Look In My Window

There is all type of windows, there are Bey windows, where you can see everything around you.
There are tall windows that allows light to come through.
There are windows that have a dark coating, so you can't see in the window.
There's a window to the soul, so walk with me and take a look in my window.
The window has I've been looking through is a spiritual window that provides me with light and insight.
So please take a look in my window.

In a spiritual sense, a window I have been looking through symbolizes new possibilities will arise.
So take a look in my window.
The eyes are the window is the of the soul.
Hope is outside the window because I no longer smoking dope.
Take a look in my window.

The soul only heals through insight and awareness.
You have to uncover, to discover to recover, so take a look out my window.
Mathew 6:22: If your eyes are good, your whole body will be filled with light. If the light within shows darkness, everything you see is in total darkness, your mind, body, and soul.

I'm truly grateful that now I have a clear vision out of my window; I no longer have fear are even be scared because now my window is clear, so take a look out of my window because now it's clear. "The fight is fixed."

Angela Brock

Whatever you're going through; however, the odds are against you; the fight is fixed. All the evil that comes at you is not of you because the fight is fixed. I no longer have to fight addiction, depression, anxiety, loneliness, being molested, being abuse. I know God is in the healing business because my life belongs to him, so I know he will fight all my battles because the fight is fixed.

Jesus took a blow for my sins Stripped from His clothing.
His body was placed on a cross,
Jesus paid the penalty for my sins for me to have a relationship with God.
So I no longer have to fight because the fight is fixed.

If You Only Knew How God Turned My Mess Into A Message

Broken but not Scattered.

The broken I'm talking about is giving up all hope, dreams and no longer in pieces.
My life is like a puzzle scattered in bits and pieces, not knowing what pieces of the puzzle fit because I was scattered and broken pieces.

God heard my cry and has been helping me to put the scattered pieces back together. I remembered being scattered around in pieces trying to find what pieces of my puzzle belongs, where darkness is all I have seen.

Feeling lost, lonely, and confused, I woundering if I mess my life up so much that I was doom. Addiction had taken over all the pain, hurt, loneliness, every part of my body, mind, and soul. I was infiltrated by the disease of addiction, cunning, powerful, patient, and lurk around lest expected.

Stole my whole identity turned me into someone I didn't know. When I look in the mirror, I saw a shadow fading away; death was around the corner, the enemy wanted my soul. Prisoner in my mind and crack-cocaine became a component. The disease told me when to sleep when to eat, when to bath, without a care in the world. Scattered in bits and pieces, but God gave me grace and mercy even when I didn't deserve it.

Now my pieces that were once scattered are now under repair. Spirits coming alive because I survive that lie. There hope after dope, pursuing my dreams build my esteem. I'm becoming the woman God wants me to be, I was once broken, but I'm no longer scattered.
Broken but not scattered

Angela Brock

Take a Walk in my Shoes

Shoes are intended to protect and comfort the human feet, but when the human feet don't have a clear path, it winds up in places no human being should ever experience.

People, Places, and things seem to be the common dominator for self-destruction. Caught up in the grip of addiction. Walk with me.

Mind consume with obsession and compulsion, crack cocaine became my lover and my friend. Take a walk in my shoes, chasing the first hit, waking up with strange men, not protecting myself, not knowing how my feet landed me in someone's bed. Take a walk in my shoes.

All my morals and values thrown out the window. In the beginning, it was for social entertainment, but here comes the pain because it became a job. I had to have it. The glass dick became my security blanket, calling my name, day in day out in a seductive way, where drugs and sex became a combo meal, couldn't have one without the other. Take a walk in my shoes. Being abused and beaten and rape by a person who said they love me. Being called a name other than my name.
Take a walk in my shoes.

God heard my cry, a heartfelt cry, and rescue me. Enough is enough. Me and my children suffered enough from the choices and decision I made. If you walk a mile in my shoes, you will praise God" too because He walks beside me. Now I'm wearing a new pair of shoes, with style and class, head-up not looking down because now I no longer have to look down with a frown
so take a walk in my shoes.

If You Only Knew How God Turned My Mess Into A Message

Scripture 1 Peter 2:21 For even hereunto were ye called because Christ also suffered for us, leaving was an angel, that yo should follow his steps
Take a walk in my shoes

Angela Brock

Not who I am, Who's I am

I was given the name Angela, an angel, a messenger of God. I always knew something was different and unique about me. I was blessed with the gift of discernment; I felt trouble; I felt other's pain but was good at hiding my own pain. I was taught never to let a person see you sweat, and I tried hard to live up to that expectation. Pain has been a motivator to seek God first because man or woman will disappoint you.
It's not who I am; it who's I am a child of God.
Scripture Roman 12:2 and be not conformed for this world be ye transformed by the renewing of the mind that and my prove what (is good, and acceptable, and perfect, will of God
"Walk like your going somewhere."

Walking is a form of taking one foot in front of another until your standing on solid ground. Walking is a form of taking you from one destination to another. Follow me walk like your going somewhere. When we were born, we are consciously aware of ourselves; we are the universe of the whole world. People, places, things around us, to fulfill all our needs, walk like your going somewhere. Anger, resentment, and fear makes up the triangle of self-obsession; total self-centeredness was my custom, to hide the pain and disappointment rather, it was by my hands are someone else's. Walk like your going somewhere. Walks can be smooth, with a clear path of self-preservation and motivation, things can be rocky with pain or despair. Choose your walk like your going somewhere. Resentment is usually from a past situation. Anger is a current situation, and fear is usually of the unknown of your future. None of these are good if you're trying to go somewhere. For many years I found myself consumed with

If You Only Knew How God Turned My Mess Into A Message

this whole triangle, which had denied me to live my full potential in life.

Today my pain has been a substitute with healing; my resentment has been placed with love; my fear has been placed with faith because today I want to walk like I'm going somewhere. My girl Mellie Mel known as Carmilla, always says walk like going somewhere.

Angela Brock

Mirror Mirror

When I look in the mirror, there's a glare, then a vision of a woman who's under repair.
Mirror mirror on the wall who's that woman staring afar,

It's me trying to find a place to be, Never feeling connected, always been rejected.
Just a little girl in this world trying to find love and acceptance in anyone's eyes.
My mama was so consumed in finding her place, by using other men for her own escape, Daddy was running a little too fast a time, chasing a dream, while my esteem became a dream.

Survival became my norm, just a little girl in this big world trying to find love in anyone's eyes.
Mirror, Mirror on the wall, I see a woman who's been through a lot of pain, hide it well, to try to disguise.
Like a spy, covering up lies, to supress the truth because it hurt so much inside.
Mirror Mirror on the wall.

I starting to like what I see, I strong black woman who has a pass, but now able to look in the mirror and see the beauty in a glass.
Glass have full but is now under repair because now I'm able to love and appreciate the woman that I see in the mirror

If You Only Knew How God Turned My Mess Into A Message

At the End of the Road

As far as I can remember, I have had a need to escape from myself and my feelings. As a child, I live in fantasy to escape from my emotions like fear, shame, guilt, inadequacy, insecurity, inferiority, and over-sensitive about everything. But I was good at masking my feelings so no one can see my vulnerability.

Because I was always living in a fantasy, I became a chameleon to be someone else than being free to be myself. I was very impulsive, never knew how my days were going to end. Chasing after a fantasy that never came true, the only thing that I know was true was that I started to lose my identity, chasing an illusion.

The drugs had imprisoned me, and addiction was like a monkey on my back. I was like a human garbage disposal, addicted to more; there wasn't any drug I didn't try to feel that void that places me in a very dark place. Most of the time, I didn't know how a made it home, waking up with strange men, barely remembering their name. Sad to say, but it's a true story. The drug had turned against me; I no longer got high, I got low, and the shame, fear, inferiority, despair, and loneliness became part of my existence.

At this point, I thought I was going to die a using addict.
Caught up in an abusive relationship, where I became immune to the abuse, which made me go deeper into addiction. If the drugs didn't kill me, the lifestyle will.

July 25, 1993, I got sick of my current situation and came to terms that I had a problem and needed some help. I tried many detoxes, rehab. Psychiatry, religion, none of these methods were sufficient, my disease always resurfaces until desperation.

Angela Brock

I found myself in Narcotic Anonymous. This was when my end of my road, I found hope. The gift of desperation lead me into the rooms, and the gift of recovery has shown me a new way to live.

If You Only Knew How God Turned My Mess Into A Message

Dealing with Rejection

Rejection is an action of dismissing or refusing, which always made me reluctant to try new things or deal with new people due to the fear of rejection.

As far as I can remember. as a little girl, I never felt connected to my peers, something was not right, being forced to mature beyond my years.

Being a child was no longer attractive to me, So I'm stuck in a child's body, but my mind was doing adult things. My peers only stuck around because I had things that many of them didn't have.

I found myself being a people-pleaser just to keep folks around. But early on, that particular defect ran its course. I became a loner because it was a lot safer to do me in fear of being rejected over and over and over.

At this time, my mom became pregnant with my baby sister "Nae" and she was diagnosed Saradosis, and being the oldest, I felt the need to help her. That's a whole other book.

Rejection went on from a child into adulthood, so I develop a defense mechanism, I'll reject you first so I won't have to feel the pain of being rejected. So the best way for me to deal with rejection is to allow myself to process what I'm feeling doesn't deny them, and express them to a support system that generally cares about me. Don't put all my eggs in one basket, because people, in general, will fail you.

It's May 30, 2020; after working an 11-to 7 am shift, I decided to go to Target to pick up something that I needed at home, I spotted a loved one. I was so glad to see her, but the feeling wasn't mutual. The feeling of rejection came over me; at first I felt hurt, but while shopping, acceptance came, then I had to express how it made me feel. What I learned about people is when someone is

Angela Brock

hurting there incapable of showing love, support, compassion because of their lock and loading in their own triangle of self-obsession.

Anger, resentment, and fear I've been there many times. It's a luxury I choose not to stay in because it brings on depression, being vindictive, spiteful, hurt people, hurt people.

You never know what people are going through; it's not my job to fix it, figure it out, or take it on. I have grown and mature spiritually and getting to know myself. I came to term, when this feeling of feeling rejected has nothing to do with me it's how that person feels towards themself.

Many are feeling insecure, while I"m feeling confidant, feeling inadequate, at the time I might be feeling the same way, inability to have self-acceptance of their situation, my job is to pray for them to find peace in themself because it helps me not to become a victim of self-rejection.

My perception of rejection has a different definition now that I got a better perspective of my life. A lot of time, I think I'm being rejecting, but God is really perfecting me from you and you from me.

If You Only Knew How God Turned My Mess Into A Message

A Woman's Worth

I've overcome everything that was attended to destroy me; a woman worth.
I rather walk alone in darkness than follow anyone else's shoes. A woman worth.

I'd rather walk in the rain with a man who treats me like a queen then ride in a Benz with a man who doesn't value me.
A woman worth.

Nobody goes through more shit than a woman that's down for the wrong man. A woman worth. When you know your worth, you don't mind being a lady in the street and a hoe in the bedroom; if a man your chasing, value your worth.
 A woman Worth.

Sometimes when you start looking at your value and your worth, a real man will appreciate your strength, your courage, your accomplishment and become an asset to your life, but a man filled with insecurities, inadequacies, and feel threatened by your circumstances can't appreciate the value of a real woman.

Being an independent female, you may feel undervalued because quiet as spoken; I don't need you; I want you. Because finally, I found my worth.

Angela Brock

Coming to Terms

Coming to terms is not an easy task; many times, I found myself in a state of denial, not wanting to accept the cards that are dealt to me.

Making excuses for other behavior on top of my behavior. Justifying and rationalizing "bull-shit" when the writing is on the wall. I realized it's going to be a special person to deal with my bullshit and what comes with me. Taking the bitter with the sweet and embracing the good with the bad.

Coming to my terms, I'm not as good as I think I am, nor bad as people see me because I'm coming to my terms. Life hasn't been easy, easy come, easy go. Sometimes folks are in your life for a season, a reason.

Season changes; there's winter, spring, and fall. I'm currently in the season of change and everyone not going to be part of this current season because I finally came to my terms.

If You Only Knew How God Turned My Mess Into A Message

Take me as I Am

Being myself means you like who you are. Being yourself means living life how you want to live, regardless of other people's opinions. It's hard to be me, but I rather be me because everyone else is taken.

I've struggled most of my life trying to fit in someone else's shoes in are circle. Found myself pleasing others so I wouldn't be judge harshly by others' opinions of me." They call that people-pleasing" a needed violation, or just to feel apart of someone's life.

It dawned on me the more I gave of myself, the more folks expect from me. Before I came into my truth, I wanted to be anyone but myself, whatever that means, but to be honest, I was searching for myself.

I realized once I continue to search for my purpose in life, I realized I had a lot of unique qualities that separate me from others. The greatest gift I discover by being me it allows me to have the courage to be myself, and I'm able to live my life how I want to live it. Take me as I am.

Being a fire sign, I realized I was strong, confidant, and standing for what I believe in; characteristic in my personality I'm loyal with most and loved by many, I always had the ability as far as I know, I've always been straight forward, I always spoke my mind, which got me a lot of jack-pots with others.

My mom uses to say to me over and over that it's not what you say. It's how you say it; because of my stubbornness, I sometime found myself on the outside looking in. Thank God for God he has allowed me to tap into my creativity to write this book about my life. I always gave people bits and pieces of myself because I was searching for me.

Angela Brock

Take me as I am. I was born to be a natural leader, but I allowed the drug to enslaved me. It was baffling, powerful, and control my whole of my entire life.

Because I suffered from total self-centerness, today I'm beginning to realized I have started to shift from self-centerness and more God-center. Take me as I am!!

If You Only Knew How God Turned My Mess Into A Message

God Plans

When I look back in my life, Every struggle, every pain, every heartache, every failure, every test, every lesson was in God's divine plan.

God can not bring you to him until he breaks you down in a humbling state. That's God Plans Psalms 57.2 "
I cry out to God most high, to God who fulfills his purpose for me. This is key to understanding God's purpose for my life. God has numbered my days and will fulfill every purpose he has for me. However, my choices and actions also matter. Life can be hard, but through trials and the story of my life.

There's something about my character loves the chase, the excitement, the fantasy, and living in an illusion; there's a bad girl who lives inside me—addicted to fantasy and the lifestyle that comes with it, lights, camera, action, I'm the main character in the movie. But the ending is not what I participated.
God's plan for my life life is not a movie with a bad ending; it's a movie with a life he chooses for me once you come to know him. That's Gods Plan!!

Angela Brock

God Forgive Me Of My Sins

God has no limited times to forgive us as long as we are not sinning intentionally, taking advantage of his
Grace in 1John 1:9, we are told that if we are sorry of our actions and towards God, then He is ready to forgive us of our sin and give grace and mercy even when we don't deserve it. The sins I'm talking about are the seven deadly sins such as greed, sloth, lust, gluttony, which can be deadly for my spiritual growth.

Greed is something I'm guilty of; when I'm lock and loaded on this particular sin, I can be very selfish, self-absorbed, and desire more, totally self-center, nothing is never enough; the more I get, the more I want and will step on anyone toes to get it.
Sloth- I don't always live in my potential; I become lazy and complacent to make any effort to better my current situation.

Lust had me waking up with strange men, trying to fill the void that God can only fill it, instant gratification, it was like a drug; my mind is dirty and desires any human contact, love me, degrading myself a lady. Gluttony- means to over-indulge-over consumption of food, drinks, wealth with items. There's time I will go on binges eating stuff that's not healthy for my body.

Trying to fill the void only: God can, trying to mask anxiety, depression, or just eating because it's there. Vanity- It's a bad one, Always been good dressing the outside but dying on the inside. Vanity is something showed on the outside, surface, and usually view as a negative, and is most defined either in terms of pride (or inflated pride). A need for things to make me feel whole are appear to be whole; insecurity is around the corner, covering up with things to the outside world like you got it all together.

If You Only Knew How God Turned My Mess Into A Message

Pride- can be deadly for me, this is when I'm easing God out and relying on my way of thinking. Pride sometimes will not allow me to express the hurt, pain, or disappointments done to me because it does come out in an unhealthy matter.

Now I'm entering into something deadly, which is resentment. Ways I been praticing in forgiving myself, it's really important to focus on my emotions, and think of each mistake has taught me a lesson, acknowledge my wrongs, and if so correct them or don't do them again.

Give myself permission to process what I'm feeling. Have a heartfelt conversation with myself and try real hard not to be too critical of myself. Quiet my mind so I can focus on the positive and not the negative, So God, I'm not perfect, but I'm perfectly made by you, let your will bedbone because I don't know any better. Forgive me of my sins.

Angela Brock

Free Yourself

Through all my trials and tribulations, The Lord makes me stronger, makes me wiser, during these times. Through this, my faith is able to grow and multiply. Roman 5:3-5 shows me that suffering produces perseverance and character, which leads to hope that allows God to pour into my heart through the Holy Spirit.

Through every test theirs a testimony, I'm still standing, every pain, I'm still standing. Every failure, I'm still standing, every struggle, I'm still standing, every lesson, I'm still standing. God is the architect of my mind, my body, and my soul. This quarantine has forced me to come to my truth; I realize I don't like being around someone all the time, I really don't like sharing my space, I'm not willing to compromise when it makes me question my happiness, settling for less than what I'm worth having. I realize money not everything if you don't feel free with the situation you are in.

Freedom not free; it's a price you have to pay. Sometimes the price is being with self. Famous music artists Fantasia said it best if you're not happy, baby go free yourself. Love I had inside has died. Just admit things are not the same. Go ahead because life is too short to free yourself.

If You Only Knew How God Turned My Mess Into A Message

Is it Sex or a Relationship

Sex is defined as when a male and a female are attracted or excited with one another and express it physically. Relationships are the way in which two or more ways people are connected and relating to one another.

For as long as I can remember, I always had a distorted perception of sex and relating. I rather avoid a simple, intimate conversation with someone I'm attracted to but rather allow my physical attraction to overwhelm a simple conversation.

Sex was never explained; at the age of thirteen, I had my first sexual encounter; this is not my first exploring experience but my first sexual encounter, but because no one told me anything about protected myself, I got pregnant; first time ever having sex. I've been pregnant five times but only have two sons.
Do the math, using abortions as a form of birth control, a warp, and distorted perception of sex.

I realized today I suffered from self-loathing, contempt for others, and abuse. Not loving myself enough to value my worth. As I begin to clear up some of the confusion and contradictions in my life, I can now move forward with less baggage and heal the little girl that abuse and mistreated her body for instant gratification that only lasted for a short period.

Here come the guilt and shame because I engaged in behaviors that conflicted with my belief to gain acceptance and love from others. Sex and drugs were like a combo meal; I couldn't have one without the other. Today at the age of 56, I know the difference between sex and a relationship so ask yourself, Am I just having sex, or am I in a relationship.

Angela Brock

Connection to Others

As far as I can remember, I always struggled to connect with others from a young girl. I always felt set apart from my peers. I felt different, and it followed me through my adulthood. Identification always made me feel connected with others.

I one of those people who don't tell me something, show me something. As a little girl, I was told when I rebel against an authority figure, mostly my mom, that I will not mount to anything, which put me in a rebellious and defiant state. I wanted attention rather it was negative or positive; that was a sense of connecting. As an adolescent into my teen years, I enjoyed dancing it took me outside myself, I would go into mesmerized and fantasize, which made me feel connected with music.

I fought all my life not to lose my individuality, so I became a chameleon just to feel connected. Having to grow up fast separated me from others. I no longer participated in kid games. All bets were off; welcome to adulthood. The streets became my playground, and that made me connected to others.

I'm now a dreamer brought into the lie that I would never amount to anything. It's funny how words can damage a child's sense of being, self-esteem, or self-worth in life, but God delivered me from self-destructive behaviors and place me in the room of NA, Never Alone; Never Again.

I felt connected with folks that suffered from a disease of addiction, I was then, and only them found a connection with myself. My spirit came alive; I no longer felt alone in society. I finally found a place that men and women gather together because drugs had been a major problem in their lives.

If You Only Knew How God Turned My Mess Into A Message

Today I no longer have to be in a group to feel connected. I no longer look at myself as a failure but a woman with character and integrity. I know I have compromised my worth in relationships to gain acceptance and love from family are friends. I no longer trust man or woman to be socially accepted because now I'm now connected to God!!!

Angela Brock

Why Do I I Stay When It's Pass the Expiration Date

Expiration has a deadline sometimes. I can stay past the expiration date. When you go into the grocery store, everything that you purchase has an expiration date, just like people in your life. Holding on because of my own selfish needs, not wanted to be alone, due to convenience and comfortability, but the relationship has expired.

People we get involve with is like an investment; it's like putting money in the bank and hopefully gain interest because you invest in it. Some investments may not be healthy for your spiritual growth. I began compromising and settling for less when I deserve more. Reality sets in, looking at what's in front of you, the writing is on the wall, denial sets in, but it's your spirit you know the relationship has expired. So I ask myself why I stay?

Longivity in any relationship kept me stuck, rather it's with an intimate relationship, friendship, family member, jobs; however, the season has changed I have to learn to adapt to the season. Some folks are in your life for season and reason. So why do I hold on when the season has changed?

Fear always questions what my spirit tells me; if I let go of these things, where would I go. When I did a fearless and moral inventory of myself, I'm the common dominator of all my dilemmas; no one can hurt me more than I can hurt myself, so my old way of thinking no longer works. It has expired. It time to stand for something are I will continue to fall for anything.

If You Only Knew How God Turned My Mess Into A Message

It's An Inside Job

When I decided to get my life back on track, I didn't know it was an inside job realizing that my outside doesn't make the pain that I hide on the inside,

It is an inside job; suffering from low-self esteem, no self-worth, being co-dependent, and living with anger, resentment, and fears. Being a survivor of abuse, being broken, not really trusting that God, who saved me from the depth of hell.

Always been good at dressing up the outside but was a walking garbage can on the inside. I didn't know at the time it's an inside job. For years I was abstinent from the drugs, still practicing those grimmy ass ways. Totally self-centered until the pain had remained the same, I did something different.

The transformation God took me through was a painful experience; it was hard to see the good in me but, God saw the best in me when everyone saw the worst in me because its an inside job. It was only when I stop having a war with myself is when the healing has begun. So much time wasted fighting a no-win situation, when all it took is for me to look inside, I can't dress it up, sex it up, because today I know it's an inside job.

Angela Brock

Awakenings

There are many awakenings; there's spiritual awakening and rude awakening, I experience both. A spiritual awakening is just that; when your spirit comes alive, when you don't do positive things to feed the spirit, it will go back to sleep. When I decided to give my life to God, that was an awakening, when I surrender to the disease of addiction, that was an awakening, when I no longer cause pain in my mothers' eyes, that was an awakening.

When I no longer wanted to die. I'm talking about a spiritual death, which was an awakening, When I no longer wake-up wondering how I'm going to get the next one, that is an awakening. When I no longer compromise my values, that's an awakening. When I no longer use manipulation to get my way, that's an awakening. When I no longer need validation from others, that's an awakening. When I let go of whatever it is because the pain remains the same, holding on is more painful, That's an awakening.

A rude awakening is when something is revealed to you through betrayal, disappointment, heartache, and it's hard to shake because it's mostly reveal through people you love. Love has always been a sensitive subject for me. I love more and give more to those I love, but the same is not given back; that's been a rude awakening. I do know that hurt people hurt people its reality, and that has been a rude awakening. Holding unrealistic expectations on folks has been an awakening. I can go on and on; awakenings have allowed to accept reality.

If You Only Knew How God Turned My Mess Into A Message

I'm Still Standing

Everything that was meant to break me, I'm still standing, I'm a woman who has fought thousands of battles. But I'm still standing. Addiction couldn't take me out; I'm still standing.

I shed many tears, I'm still standing, my heart has been broken, I been betrayed, abandoned, rejected, but I still walk proud because I'm still standing.

If it don't kill me, all it can do is make me stronger because I'm still standing; I'm a woman who loves hard even when it's not given back but guess what? I'm still standing.

I'm learning to walk through my fears, never regreting my past. Forgiving those who cause me harm, confessing my wrong to God. I am making amends when it is possible, except when to do so would injure them or others.

If God don't give me anything else, he's allowed me to accept my imperfection, to embrace my scars, and to be okay with the woman I see. I make room for improvement because I'm still standing.

Angela Brock

Giving Myself Permission to Take Care of Myself

For a long time, my goal was to make sure you were happy, to fix your problem, and to make sure your emotion was taken care of but denying myself to do the same for me. I found out it's important that I surround myself around people who will not allow me to stay in my sickness of co-dependency, people pleaseing, attention seeking, compromising, and settleing less than I deserve.

Today I'm giving myself permission to feel what I feel, to stop denying what's in front of me, to embrace who I am, and to allow myself permission to let go when necessary.

I allow myself to be okay with my uniqueness, never was comfortable with clicks, always needed to be free to be myself. I always denied myself to live my potential afraid of failure and also a success. It's important for me to live in the moment, never projecting my future, but plan for my future, walk by faith and not by sight; the spirit is healing from all the bruises I endured, allowing me to take care of myself mentally, emotionally, physically, and spiritually. I'm going through a surgery of the spirit.

If You Only Knew How God Turned My Mess Into A Message

Amends and Reconciliation

As I began to mature, my behaviors have changed. Far from perfect, still room for improvement. Recognizing the chaos and confussion, I cause in myself and others allows me to take another look. Sometimes, the damage I cause has been difficult for others to forgive, but asking God to forgive me from all the guilt, shame, and remorse don't keep me trapped in self-destruction.

But it doesn't begin or end just because I'm able to identify my wrongs and harm I may have cause takes more than just admitting it; it comes to changing the behaviors. There might be folks that will never forgive me; what's important that I forgive myself. Making direct amends is crucial; when I began to clean-up my side of the street, I feel it's easier for me not to take on or feel obligated to clean up the up their part of the street. God is in the forgiving business; my job is not to take a magic wand and heal a person's heart; that's God's job; my job is to pray, admit my wrong, and God will do the rest.

Angela Brock

It's Necessary To Be Me Because Everyone Else is Taken

I have a buddy who always makes this statement:
"It's necessary to be me because everyone else been taken," very witty, wise, and clever with the tongue. Have knowledge beyond her years, ran the same streets, connected with the same people but never ran into one another. I call her G.
Much older than I, I always gravitated to an older and wiser woman than myself. Being me has had many challenges; I'm not clicking, I'm a loner, free spirit, always been adventurous, a chameleon can blend in any situation I encounter, and be around any type of race just blend.

I guess that has always been a gift for me. When I meet G on this new way of living, I had to know her, you talking about funny there's never a dull moment with her. When I'm feeling low, she doesn't allow me to go too low, always had the ability to see the bright side of a situation, that's G. We rarely barely see eye to eye, but because of the love and respect for each other, our friendship stays alive that's my buddy G.

G hides behind sarcasm that hides her fear, just like me. I believe God has a way to put folks in your life; emotionally, she was always available. A quick story my mom was dying, and my best friend was making frequent trips to the hospital, my son was incarcerated, had custody of my grandson, and my marriage was just existing. Most of the time, I didn't know if I was coming or going; what I did was I wasn't going to get high no matter what was going on. This is only one of many incidents that we supported one another through life devastating incidents. I held that true to my heart, and I will never forget so saying that it's

If You Only Knew How God Turned My Mess Into A Message

necessary to be me because everyone else has been taken. That speaks volumes in my life; all I ever wanted to be is me; if I died today and came back, I want to be me that's something she deposits in , to be free to be me.

Angela Brock

My Shero

Meet her going on 17 years ago, it was like God connected us together, even though we meet through a mutual friend, she became my sister, my family, my confidant, and most definitely my strength. I watch and witness God take you from a no-win situation, heal you, stood you up; you are my shero. I couldn't ask for a better example of a woman who walks by faith and not by sight; you are my shero.

When I complain about fixable things, and I watch you being under the care of, you are my shero. Friends are hard to find and rare to connect with. I'm so glad God choose you for me because you are my shero. Love you, Deb

If You Only Knew How God Turned My Mess Into A Message

Having a Better Perspective of My Life

My life was given to me by God. God is my father, the Holy Spirit is my mother, and God chooses my parents to be my guardian. There's time I took my life for granted, playing Russian Roulette with my life. Putting myself in a situation that life and death was around the corner. Finding a better perspective of my life. We all live, and we all are going to die. Life did not promise; it's what you do with your life counts. So get a better perspective of your life. Life can be like an emotional roller coaster; there are ups and downs, turn-around the question is will you be able to abstain from the ride? So get a better perspective of your life.

Where in the times not knowing how the days are going to begin or end. So get a better perspective of your life. Life is not promised, so make it right with the people you love, you cheerish, and embrace the memories you share because tomorrow is not promised. Get a better perspective of your life.

Angela Brock

Mr. Wrong

Mary J Blige said it perfectly, "Bad boys are no good, and good boys are not fun." There a bad girl that lives inside of me. This is the story of my life. Choosing men with the same defect I have, emotionally unavailable, street-smart, go-getter, hustler, and true to the Game. Didn't know that games have an ending. Addicted to money, property, and prestige, and also pain. Finding potentials in anyone I got involve with. Dress them up, sex them up, to emotional fuck me up. Always been a dream chasers, but you know about dreams. Eventually, you have to wake up. Reality set in, start evaluated how you got there.

Damm, I did it again, over and over again, until the pain outweight the pleasure. Now that I'm older, my mind needs to be stimulated, and my body will follow. Being in something that physically the person is there, but you're still alone. Going from loving intimacy. Into Me loving every being of yourself to taking a risk to love again. Now I'm in a place what love got to do with It. Love is an emotion in that you show compassion, compromising, giving of yourself, even if your spirit doesn't feel it. You stay because of the convenience. Is it worth it to have someone when love don't live there anymore? Compromising your value and your moral for someone who don't appreciate it, how do I continue to choose Mr. Wrong.

If You Only Knew How God Turned My Mess Into A Message

Life is An Adventure

An adventurous life does not always mean traveling, social activities with family and friends; it means taking a risk by leaving a little piece of you behind in all those you meet along the way; knowing your dreams and following them is a real adventure of life. For as long as I can remember, I have always been adventurous; looking and searching for something is someone to fill the void inside me. Rather it was people, places, or things I found myself still searching for. When I feel something is missing from my life but still not happy, I'm missing an adventure. God has taken me to a place in my life that whoever I meet its always been an adventure; any place I travel, it was an adventure, But the biggest adventure I had is being introduced to myself.

In Bible John 3:16-17 states," For God so loved the world, that he gave his only Son, that whoever believes in him should not perish but have eternal life. For God did not send his Son into the world to condemn the world, but in order for that, the world might be saved through him." I believe God put me on earth to have the adventure to touch those lives I encounter so when my day comes to be with him. Folks can say it was an adventure knowing her. So life has been an adventure.

Angela Brock

Unresolved Issues

Unresolved issues are something that hasn't been settled, brought to any type of resolution its unaddressed emotions, such as anger and sadness that extend from childhood into adulthood, which has an unhealthy feeling for your future to live happy, joyous, and free.

One of my biggest issues is suppressing what I'm really feeling, kicking shit under the rug like it doesn't exist. Maybe it will get better, but the issue still stands because it's unaddressed where I allow people to manipulate me. Will their presents back in my life for the same thing to happen over and over again.

And it's because of unresolved issues. For as long as I remember, every relationship I let go rather it's intimate relation, friendship, whatever ship. The people are different, the faces are different, the situation is different, but the feeling is still the same. I love people, but their love is never the same. I support folks, but I never get the same support. I allow folks to step on my heart and emotion like a doormat, and I still keep them in my present for love and acceptance. I continue to allow people to hurt my feeling, never address it like it never exists, and that's an issue. I continue to allow folks to reject me in others' presents; that's an issue. Issues are like tissue; they always pop-up. God timing is in his time; when the student is ready, the teacher will appear I think I'm ready to address my issues.

I have to learn to discern who's there to enhance my present are who there to destroy my existence. Most of the time I'm well aware of people's actions, but I ignore them like they're going to go away, but they never do; that's an issue. Anything unresolved within our energy will keep manifesting itself in our physical,

If You Only Knew How God Turned My Mess Into A Message

mental, emotional, and spiritual life will continue to pop up until I heal from it. There is no way to escaping it when I find myself saying and doing things out of my character because I'm feeling hurt, disregarded, not being treated like I treat you, and comes out in an unloving and uncaring way. It's an issue. I haven't addressed it; that still shows its rare head when that particular feeling comes up. It's an issue, so that means it to me.

So I think I'll address my issue because they continuously keep popping up like tissue because I still have unresolved issues.

Angela Brock

Out with the Old in with the New

There are four seasons Winter, Spring, Summer, and Fall. I'm in the season of spiritual enlightenment. We live two lives, we live life in our thoughts, and we live life as our experiences of the present moments.

Freedom from ourselves comes from learning how to balance thoughts and feelings in the present moment. So you got to let go of the old to embrace new things, so new possibilities can arise. So out with the Old so you can embrace the new.

When you're in the season for the spiritual insight, it takes you to a place of reinventing yourself because the old way of thinking is no longer working. The old way of behaving isn't working; your old attitude has to be renewed and replaced with something spiritual.

My old ways stop working its time to re-event a new creature, so I have to be willing so God can renew me like new. Old things I keep holding on memories, all of them wasn't all bad, People, places, and things were the common denominators, disappointment, some joy, some pain, some heartaches, but all was needed to grow into my truth and puts a flame back into my exist and allows me to get in touch with, so the spiritual it can open doors that only God has the power to do, close doors for something new to come in.

Out with the old in with the new. Doing new things is like being on an adventure, changing old places, get reacquainted with new faces; when you familiar with relationships, it's difficult to let go because it's not familiar. It's like dumping out your trash and baggage that's no longer needed to grow spiritually. But it's most important not to go back into the baggage that causes familiar pain. Out with the old end with the new.

If You Only Knew How God Turned My Mess Into A Message

Aging

It's no way to escape aging. Aging is defined as the length of time a being or thing has existed; length of life or lived' length of life or existence to the time spoken of or referred to aging which you start looking at your mortality. You start asking yourself, when am I going to die because theirs no escape from it.

Being forgetful is a sign of aging; lack of energy is a sign of aging, body aches, and pain. Sexual drive decreases is a sign of aging, weight gain and keeping it off is a sign of aging, Skin discoloration is a sign of aging. Needing to take frequent naps is a sign of aging. Losing hair is a sign of aging. Being aware of your spiritual side is a sign of aging because now you're looking at your mortality.

Growing old has made me look at the reality of things; I start asking myself, myself what have you done to enlighten your life quality? Have you did everything you needed to do, live your life to the fullest? Aging gracefully, some mild medical condition that can get better once I surrender to my own will.

Life has been good; there's has been some up and down, there's has been some moments of success, but I stayed humble. There were some moments that there was a need to change my circle of friends, but Im grateful. The most powerful thing that has happened through aging and maturing, it's important to have folks around you that deposit life, not death, in my spirit.

I welcome aging because it allows me to tap into the window that God has deposited into me. Thank you, God, for allowing me to age with grace and with wisdom.

Angela Brock

Is It Worth the Investment

In life, we meet people from all walks of life that touch your life in a way that touches the heart. Mostly to learn valuable lessons. Are they there to enhance your life, put a flame in your spirit, support you to chase your dreams, enhance your growth, help you go through your doubts, and support you through new possibilities?

If not there not worth the investment. If you allow people to make more withdrawals than deposits in your life. You will be out of balance and in a negative. Know when to close your account because it's an investment.

Investment can be risky because you never know the outcome because you're taking a risk. Always been a risk-taker made a good decision and bad decision in life. I thank God for me having another opportunity to make some new mistakes. Is it worth the investment? I use to look at mistakes as a bad thing, especially when it comes to my heart, letting someone know me personally because it leaves me vulnerable to be hurt, disappointed, resentful, so is it really worth the investment.

The investment I'm talking about is devoted all my time, my energy, to someone that knows nothing about an investment. I find myself connected with folks with mind games, manipulated like there the victim of a situation, and try to convince you that the cause of the insecurities is lack of trust, but the bottom line there not trustworthy. Is it worth the investment?

Due to my ability to have a high tolerance for pain, I continuously find myself in a bad situation that causes me to build a wall around my heart. Is it worth an investment? I'm not just talking about one particular person, majority rules, I'm tired of investing

If You Only Knew How God Turned My Mess Into A Message

with takers, and I'm a giver. Something doesn't measure up; I find myself continuing to having a negative balance because I waste so much time investing in folks instead of investing in myself. Is it worth the investment? I"m at a point in my life that I need to seek out people who willing to deposit and no withdrawal; it's no longer worth the investment. I have been blessed with the Gift called discernment; I need to listen to the quiet voice *from God, stop investing in people, places, or things start investing in myself because I'm worth the investment…*

Angela Brock

Co-Dependency No more

Co-dependency is a characteristic of excessive emotional or psychological reliance on a partner, typically one who requires support due to illness or addiction. In my case, it started as a little girl, supported and taking care of folks. It brought me a validation to be there for someone else and continue through adulthood. I always love seeing someone else happy I found gratification in this. Didn't know this particular defect in my character would cause me a lot of heartaches, especially when I needed someone.

Even though addiction I made sure nobody was left out without getting high, I made shit happen. I didn't realize that your happiness meant more to me than my own. For as long as I remember I people's pleasing became apart of my character. Just love me, don't leave me, so I compromise my happiness for yours.

I remember being up with a still-suffering addict, sentenced to kick the habit, and when I thought it was unbearable for them, I would get them some dope. Let me clarify this when it got so unbearable for me to watch, cope for them, and take the dis-ease that was nodding at my spirit.

I remember being an adolescent taking on a role of a caretaker of my siblings; I love them like they were my own, made sacrifices that only a mother would make. Like lie for them to protect from harm's way, taking in my sister because she didn't have anywhere to go, but suffering having her there, we were both caught up in the disease of addiction. Staying in relation long past the expiration date, knowing in my soul it was unhealthy, my thinking was I invested in them, I'll fix them, and need to say I needed to be fixed.

If You Only Knew How God Turned My Mess Into A Message

Many disappointments, heart-broken, abandon, rejected by most, I finally, at the age of 56 to let go and let God. At first, it was hard to let go, but as time went on, it was easier to love those who love me, be there for those who are there for me, stop volunteering myself to show up when it's not wanted.

Allowed those who I love and would die for to have their own experience and not try to fix the situation. Life lesson makes you evaluated who love you unconditionally when you don't have anything to offer them. So today I check my motives and expectation of others because people will always feel you. I'm healing from wanted to be needed by others and evaluate what I need.

Co-dependency No-More

Angela Brock

Self-Acceptance

In the Bible, Ephesians 2:8 states, "For by the grace you have been saved through faith. And this is not your own doing; it is the gift of God." Self-Acceptance is the act of accepting oneself, the act or state of understanding and recognizing one's own abilities and limitations. I never knew my limitation; there was no limit. It was a vicious cycle of being who I thought I was and became who you wanted me to be—a chameleon blending and being who I needed to be at that particular time. If I was around folks that didn't seem real intelligent, I would dumbing-up to fit in, afraid to show that I knew a little something. So I found myself searching and seeking to find myself.

Once I came to the realization that being myself is more rewarding. I no longer have to be what you wanted me to be for violation; once I came to my truth, the road became narrow because I was no longer pleasing you and losing me.

Self-acceptance is an ongoing process; the longer I get to know myself, the wiser I become, more awareness of what makes me tick, the more folks around are weeded out. It's a lonely process to rediscover who you are; the good, the bad, and the indifference. I realize today that I'm sociable but also like being in my own space. I really don't have to be around a lot of folks to define who I am. There was a time that being around a lot of people made me feel whole and accepted. Today I accept Angie for Angie even through my imperfection, I'm perfectly made in God's eyes.

If You Only Knew How God Turned My Mess Into A Message

Am I, My Sister Keeper

14 months apart, but look identical in features. Everyone use to call us twins, but she was my best friend, my blood, my sister. Did everything together, had each other back, I was the out-going, out-spoken one, and my sister was quiet and reserved. Am I my sister keeper?

When one hurt, the other one felt it, like we were both in the wound together. Inseparable as kids into adolescence, until we gain our own circle of friends, I enjoyed dancing; she was active in sports. Both had a tom-boyish way; I like girly stuff, and she preferred things boys played with. Am I my sister keeper?

Now where adults, but both fascinating with the lifestyle of the streets, and true to the mother-fucken game, hustler by nature, all about the benjamins.

Every year we spent our summer with family in New York, where the game was introduced. Both just little girls, playing grown ladies business not knowing there a price playing grown people games. We were very protective of one another until jealousy showed its true head because our bond and interest had changed. She wanted what I had; betrayal became the demise of our relationship, but *love* kept us together. Sisters before niggers because I'm my sister keeper.

Spiritually connected, I start reflecting. Am I my sister's keeper? 11/13/1996 twenty-four years ago, the angel of death took my friend, life was never the same, I felt my sister's spirit leaving me, and God called her name. Lost and lonely and didn't know what to do, but God said, my child, live the legacy that your sister wasn't able to do. Am I my sister keeper?

Angela Brock

Sis, you planted the seed, and God has been watering all my needs. I'm clean and becoming serene because you plant that first seed. Am I my sister keeper?

If You Only Knew How God Turned My Mess Into A Message

Little Sister

Fifteen years apart, when I first saw you, I fell in love; you where a bundle of joy. I love you like you were my own. There's nothing in the world I wouldn't do for you because you were my baby sister.

Babies grow-up come into their own, develop their own identity, their own friends, and their own way of thinking. Very strong-will, very opinionated, stubborn, intelligent go-getter, these are some traits you got from me. When I went to God and asked him to take care of you, I made the hardest decision in my entire life. You were not just my sister. You were like my daughter; somewhere down the line, the roles switch due to our mother's illness, I became your surrogate mom. Never wanted you to feel the pain I felt growing up, but everybody has to learn their own lessons in life.

I was force to let you go, like a bird forcing their babies out of the nest, and I must say you soar like an eagle. I have always been proud of you for all your accomplishments; I would brag about you among my peers; they knew how much I love you because you're my Lil Sister.

I know there was a time I wasn't the most positive role-model due to my addiction, so I want to apologize for that; you needed someone to look up to, so I can imagine you felt alone, mom sick, and big sisters caught up in the disease of addiction. I pray that you find happiness in yourself; until then, nothing will make you happy. Holding on to resentments is like eating poison and expecting the person you resent to die, which is very unhealthy. Just like my kids were loan to me, and so were you. I think I'll let God handle this I love you, Lil Sis.

Angela Brock

Lil Brother

It's a true statement a mother raises their daughter but loves their son. You were the apple of our mom's eyes; her namesake Darrell spelled Darryl. Spoiled rotten by the females all your life and I was guilty of it. You have a style that people gravitate to your charisma and your out-going personality. A people person, well-liked, a lady-man, well dress and groom, But their a side of you that you avoid confrontation, just want everybody to get along and that's not reality. You hide your feeling to protect yourself, but on the flip-side, you're very sensitive. I must admit mom's death made you come into your man-hood. All of us were a big enabler.

There's the thing I shouldn't have exposed you to, like the game of hustling, and I apologize for that. I only gave you what I had, but I also love you to death; you were my Lil brother. You're all grown-up now, have a family of your own; you didn't turn out too bad Lil bro. I'm proud of you, overcame many obstacles that were meant to destroy you, even when you have done things that I should have resented you, I love you little brother

If You Only Knew How God Turned My Mess Into A Message

Sisterhood A Reunion of the Heart

The heart is a part of our body that is fragile, that loves, that hurts, that needs surgery of the spirits that were once damaged. Building a sisterhood relationship with other women was risky because the women who were such an inspiration in my life transition, like my grandmother, my mom, and my sister, and thinking of them bring me sadness, some joy, and happiness when I think of the time I spent with them.

The teaching of my grandmother gave me wisdom. The strength my mother instilled in me as a young woman. The unconditional love I received from my sisters, knowing they both had my back, whatever the situation and circumstances were, we were there for each other. Women play so many roles and wear many hats. Mother, grandmother, someone's sister, mentors, someone's wife or lover, were nurturing, teachers, guardians, enforcer, breadwinner, advisor, etc. to benefit and mentor each other just as much as we help others of our perfectly flawed circle.

I was thinking about what a sisterhood is and what exactly does it mean to me. I believe it's a bond between females that goes beyond blood ties. It's a security blanket for each female in that sisterhood in which each thread that creates that blanket defines the depth of the sisterhood.

Unfortunately, security blankets can be easily tattered with one snag of a teeny tiny thread that depreciates the value of the blanket until that small snag becomes a run, then a hole, until finally that security blanket can no longer shield you from the pain of the outside world. I think that same can be said for false sisterhoods.

Angela Brock

I truly believe you won't know the meaning of true sisterhood until what you thought was your security blanket has been taken away from you.

My vision of sisterhood would be something you never outgrow. My vision would be a connection that could be mended to be better than new if ever broken. My sisters could never be replaced but will forever evolve and uplift one another not only in times of sorrow but also in times of rejoicing.

I believe sisterhood relationships should always be honest and truthful, even when it hurts because what we *need* is not always what we want. A sisterhood relationship should be nonjudgmental confidants who can empathize and offer positive even when the resolution to whatever problem may have arisen is not always clear.

The sisterhood will be a gathering of very different women from all walks of life as we are all unique and have something to offer the world that other sisters can benefit from. To be unique is to have character, and my sisterhood may be accused of something but boring and dull wouldn't be any of them. I take pride in my sisterhood in being authentic because we as sisters can't be anything else but real.

Yes, I said in the beginning, perfectly flawed, that there is always room to grow, which is what our sisterhood is for. To help each other grow to be even better, beautiful human beings than we already are. To help each other get closer to God as well as our loved ones. To be the angel on your shoulder, always whispering positive words of encouragement. To remind each other that we are women of our word-to say what you mean and mean what you say and then do it. To help each other let go of resentment

If You Only Knew How God Turned My Mess Into A Message

and pain that eats at our souls. To be each other's security blanket. Sisterhood A Reunion of the Heart

Angela Brock

Being a Single Mother To My Two Sons

Being a single mom has been challenging and had a big impact on both of my son's life. It's a true statement a mother raises their daughter and loves their sons. It was just my boys against the world and me. I have always been a hustler by nature, so of course, my sons pick up that trait. I often use different tactics to discipline my sons. Today I know it wasn't a healthy tactic. I often use intimidation and verbal abuse to control them when they acted out in masculine ways. Psychologically I emotionally abuse them.

My firstborn Jyjuan always gravitated to overbearing, dominant, emasculating, and damage women who came off hostile. My Jy was always an overachiever, loving, caring but made bad choses by being rebellious and made bad choices in women, which made him a damaged man; the women had the same defects I had.

My second son Jaylon survived at a young age that no one is going to abuse him. It showed in his actions and behavior, a loner, not emotionally available, and very protective over those he loves shows an uncaring demeanor, which is also unhealthy to find true happiness.

I'm so sorry sons, I thought I was showing you love; I was actually hindering you two to make your own decision and mistakes; I always made the blow easier and softer. When I thought I was protecting you, I was enabling both of you. No manual tells me how to raise young men, so I apologize for my mistakes, but everything I did was always out of love.

If You Only Knew How God Turned My Mess Into A Message

Dear Momma

I know a lot of times I didn't show my gratitude for you giving me life. I have many characteristics that you carry, being the oldest, family-oriented, very protective over my cubs, strong will, loyal to the ones we love even when they're not loyal to us. The woman you overcame many obstacles, that I don't know if I was placed in the situation, would be able to overcome them.

I know today you can only give me what you had. Having me an impressable age of 17 and 18, you had my sister, neither one of wanted for nothing. You guided and provided for us to the best of your ability. A lot of choices I made on my own, I was well aware of the consequences. I think I'll let you off the hook. No, you weren't one of the most emotional and affectionate people I needed, but I knew you love me; it a bond that only a mother and daughter has.

When God called you home, it was at a part of my life, I was able to show you how much I loved you and cared about you.
Labor of love came in its right season.

Woman, you were the Rock of the family who deserves a grammy. You kept the family together, but when the angel of death called you home. None of us could ever fill the shoes you walk in; they were too big to fill. Many heartaches, disappointment, I endured, and vice-versa. I made you have many sleepless nights due to my rebellious ways, but you love me through all that; I'm truly grateful to call you my mom, which made me the woman I become.

Angela Brock

Strong, determined, nobody in my entire life can ever define a mother's love in words. It is just something one can feel, one could embrace. At the end of the day, you're still my mom, who will stand by your side and do whatever necessary to protect, die for your babies; that's who my momma was.

A diamond with many flaws but so much courage that she passed it down to her children. I am so proud to call you my mom. Rest easy, lady, because I miss you so much, Dear Momma

If You Only Knew How God Turned My Mess Into A Message

Words from the Heart to My Dad.

When I think of saying goodbye, I never thought it would be this soon: but I knew. Your body was weary, and I'm going to miss you. No man in my life will ever measure up to you. But you showed me what a good man is supposed to do. Dad, I thank you for all you have done: Especially helping me with my two sons. Dad, I want to thank you for my forty-seven years. But I must be honest, I can't stop the tears.

Dad, whatever you didn't do for me when I was young, you made it up to me three-folds by helping me raise my sons. Dad, why didn't you tell us that you were sick? Not that I could've of help you medically, but I could've supported you through it. Dad, I watched your body slowly fade away; in my mind, I asked God, "When will be the day?"

Dad, I'm grateful I did everything you asked, even though I knew it was too late. I knew God was opening up the gate. Dad, I had to share you with other people who love you so much. Dad, we didn't conversate much, but our eyes and spirit always connect.

Dad, you gave me some gifts that money or material things could never touch. You gave me the gift of compassion, unconditional love, forgiveness, family, creativity. These are just a few gifts mentioned that meant so much. So to the family that Dad loves so much, Get in touch with the gifts that Dad gave you that no one can touch. Dad, tell my mom, Rainey, Corrine, and Newt I said, what's up.

Angela Brock

This makes me look at my own mortality and wonder when my time is up. Dad, I was trying to describe. Rev. Melvin Jackson got it just perfect. You're a small piece of leather well put together. Dad, I know I'm not alone and that I have five guardian angels that were selected. So I know me, my kids, and my grandkids are well protected. Dad, I'm your last seed, and I promise to carry on your legacy.

Written by your daughter Angie

If You Only Knew How God Turned My Mess Into A Message

Family

Faces that is always memories and images of lost years

My definition of family is people you love and love back, not necessarily blood or biological, but you trust them, and they trust you, and they take care of you, and you take care of them.

Families like a reunion of the heart, a spirit that cannot be unfolded. Family is like a security blanket; unfortunately, security blankets can be easily tattered with one snag of a teeny tiny thread that depreciates the value of the blanket can no longer shield the family bond. I'm not saying my family is perfect. We are strong-willed, stubborn, bullheaded, opinionated, prideful, but we persevere through a crisis or any obstacles we encounter; that's what gives us our strength, and I'm proud of being a part of my imperfect family.

My mother was the rock of the family; when there was a dispute, she became all of our security blankets, she loved us unconditionally, she protected us to the best of ability, if there was a family member that we didn't know, she would open her house up and invite them in with open arms.

Family can also hold resentments that will eat at your soul and never have the opportunity to mend those wounds. I believe we are each other security blanket until it is taken away. My vision of family would never outgrow. My vision would be a connection that would be mended to be better than new if ever broken. A family should always be honest and truthful to one another even when it hurt because what we need is not always what we want. Granddad, 25 years ago, I was in total darkness and despair due to my addiction, and you were my security blanket. In the beginning, I thought I was there for you because my mother would

Angela Brock

have wanted me to be, but God revealed to me that I'm there because of me I can never express the gift you gave me is you help me get my life back. You believe in me when I was incapable of believing in myself.

Miss you and Love you, Grandad.

If You Only Knew How God Turned My Mess Into A Message

My Upbringing; Reflecting On My Childhood

Grew up in the era of the boomer babies in 1946 and 1964, I was born in 1964. In this particular generation, we experience some of the most important events in American history. Politically, the Civil Rights Movement and the Vietnam War all were affected by the baby boomer, too young to know what was really going on. Still, the growth in families grew tremendously; a lot of my friends had 5 are 6 siblings in one household; it was just me and my sister Rainey. We attended A Lee O' Weil Elementary; this is when my curiosity the sneakiness creep in, I use to tell my teacher I needed to go to the bathroom, where I snuck out to go to the store, buy candy to eat during the recession. Center Avenue, Wylie Avenue was attractive to me. Just a little girl trying to find something is someone to fill the void I felt inside.

Growing up in the Projects Elmore Square, the village looked over their youth. My mom lived in a two-bedroom apartment, 2146 Elmore Square 3rd floor; I can remember it like it was yesterday. The decor wasn't real fancy, floral prints, nothing matching, but it was liveable and clean; my sister and I didn't want for anything. Always food on the table, clean clothes, I mostly what we wanted and everything we needed. My mom denied herself to make sure we didn't do without. This is the time case-workers used to visit your home in order for you to get assistance from Welfare. I used to see my mom hiding certain things from the caseworker so she can continue getting assistance to take care of my sister and me. My mother had us very young me at the age of 16, and when she graduated, she already had two kids. My father wasn't around as much, he and my mother had already separated.

I looked forward to the summer, the fire hydrant was turned on, those hot and summery days. I love it. Playing with my peers, I

Angela Brock

spy, Release the Den at the Hypo, which was directly behind the building I lived at. Every weekend there would be block parties, families took turns sponsoring it, but everyone in the community would contribute something towards the festivities. Hot dogs, hamburgers, shaved ice balls, cotton-candy, big bags of peanuts, popcorn, games like water balloon tossing, potato sack race, and more, we just had a good time.

My mom would support card parties, sell dinners; this went on all weekend. Every Sunday, my sister and I went to church with my great-aunt, who I always acknowledge as my grandmother because she raised my mother and was always was in my life. We went to this Catholic Church right across from Freedom Corner; there was a caucasian couple who adopted my sister and me through the church, through Angle Tree. Every birthday, every holiday, my sister and I had two of everything. We were truly blessed to never be without or do without this family supporting my sister and me.

West View Park was the main attraction for the people who live in the Hill District we had a yearly picnic. Families pack up their picnic basket with fried chicken, potato salad, watermelon, and we congregated like one happy family, from sun up to sundown. At this time, my mother was furthering her education at CCAC for education. She found out she was pregnant with my only brother; this was when my grandmom Corrine, my Newky, and my mom decided to move from a place where my childhood memories, child-hood friends, were going to replace them with new memories, new friends, my life change. I'm now 10 years old, attending a new school, making new friends, but I'm so grateful I had my sister Rainey to walk through my fears. Madison Elementary is the school-Monkey Madison; that's what they called it because of the Monkeys engraved outside the building.

If You Only Knew How God Turned My Mess Into A Message

New Beginning (Childhood)

The community we moved to a considered middle class, Schenley Heights, a lot of African Americans brought homes there; this was a new adventure, new community, new friends. Still, I always found my way back to Elmore Square to visit my old friends. As time went on, I got connected with new associates; dancing has always been my thing, it took me out of myself. Our home was a duplex; the first floor is where my grandmom Corrine and Newky stayed; one bedroom, kitchen, living room, bath, and basement were all connected. The aroma that flowed through our house on the weekends was striking, fried apples and cinnamon, buttermilk biscuit, and scramble-egg with cream-style corn. I spent a lot of time on the first floor, with a pile a the foot of my grandmother's bed. It was cozy and warm; even though I had my own room that I shared with my sister Rainey, I always found myself at the foot of my grandmother's bed. We got up every morning; I assisted her with whatever meals we were going to eat for today.

The second floor in the duplex was where my mom stayed, me and my sister Rainey had the whole attic; it was one large room and a small room connected that I made our living room area, with the strobe-lights, nets on the ceiling, small couch, a small coffee table. This was the room we entertain our company, our women's cave area. It was like our own apartment away from the rest of the house. Mom rarely came upstairs, so you know, all kind of stuff was jumping on up there. Sneaking boys throw the window, which I also use the same exit to enter in and out of the house, without my mother knowing, especially when I was on punishment.

Angela Brock

Middle school was when my curiosity of boys and drug experimenting started, that when we started making freguent trips to the Big Apple, I became fascinated with the streets. New York was a city that never sleeps, always something going on, day in and day night.

My sister Rainey and I had found a place in the World, love the hustle and bustle of the Big Apple. My Auntie took us on frequent trips to Coney Island, an amusement park that was famous Mr. Pop Burger, and their roller coaster, the Cyclone. My sister and I look forward every summer to visit my auntie, Julia. This was when we got familiar with the latest fashion. Pittsburgh was beginning to be too slow for my sister's fast past activities, and I was accustomed to it. Because we travel on Greyhound, we would purchase marijuana to sell once we hit the Burg. This went on for years; hustling became second nature, my curiosity became more vivid but was real good hiding it from my mom.

As long as I kept my grades up, it was easy to hide what I have done in the streets. Our home was the hang-out place where all our friends hung-out; my mom was famous for her Koolaide, everybody in the neighborhood loved her Koolaide. They still talk about it today. Rainey and I would have socials, my mom would cook, that women loved to cook, which made us very popular in our community.

Now the little girl in me is now participating in grow-up activities, so dancing became second nature; it was now an illusion. The people I hung with became second, and men and drugs and partying were my priority. Just thirteen, the first sexual experience I got pregnant, my innocence was taken away in the blink of an eye. Hide it well.

If You Only Knew How God Turned My Mess Into A Message

Addiction

Addiction showed its rare head; now I'm addicted to the lifestyle, the behaviors that came with it, manipulating and justifying my behavior, and I'm just in middle school getting ready for high school. Look in loaded in self-destruction and didn't even know it. Now I'm going to bars because I no longer felt a connection with my peers. I wore many masks. A little incident girl at home, but something I didn't know in the evening. Center Avenue at that time reminded me of baby Harlem, New York. There were stores on every corner. Benny Diamond had everything; it was the black people's bank to cash check. Hicks Superette is where we brought our groceries; there were bars on every corner, and Terrance Hall had an old fashion ice cream parlor where I brought banana splits and milk shakes. The Blue room was the main attraction where all the pimps and hoes and drug dealers would hung-out. Now there's Herron Avenue, Hank and Don's, Jimmy's Bar, Swartz Superette, Boykins, who was famous for their chicken; the bakery had the largest cookies in Pittsburgh owned by Ms. Grace. I'm just a little girl trying to find her place; I was in heaven.

Many secrets were hidden behind the doors at 3369 Milwaukee street. I was always told what goes on in the house stays in the house; of course, I broke that rule with my rebellion and anger. Men had become my momma's priority, bringing strange men, they never stayed long; she was chasing a dream that was breaking her self-esteem. I promise to God that I would never stupidly fall in love with a man. Mothers should never bring strange men around their grow-up girls; temptation always lurks around, curiosity is around the corner, a person that preys on your girls show-up shatters a young girl's life and follows them through adulthood. At one time, was a victim now becoming a volunteer due to not feeling worthy of love, self-respect for yourself,

Angela Brock

compromising all your morals and values, just for instant-gratification. **Don't know the difference of being love or being in lust**

I was never really connected with females unless they were a lot older than me; I was a junior in high school but was hanging with seniors. I tried out for many things like the Pom- Pom Girls, was accepted, but my connection with females wasn't accepted. I was never the one for clicks, always did my own thing, so my interest in becoming apart of a group vanish quickly. To be honest, it was interfering with my hustling; I started off selling joint, you know the saying graduated to a bigger thing, now I'm taking paper acid, cocaine, a little heroin but was still was hiding an addiction. Addiction is such a cunning enemy that disguises itself as normal, but deep inside, you lose yourself.

Emotionally I wasnt growing to be a productive member of society; I just exist. I was going with the flow of life, missing out on opportunities that could make me a better person. I thought I was too smart for my own good; the lies I told myself,
"*I'm okay, I can handle this, it's just for social entertainment, and it's social acceptability,*" all led to disaster.

I did find time to go to business school after graduating from high school to please my mom's needs. I graduated with a Bradford Business School certificate for Retail Management; I wanted to be a buyer for department stores. I took little jobs doing inventories, sales associates but never had an opportunity to become a buyer; you had to know someone inside to survive in this industry.

Heartbroken from my high school sweetheart and a close friend, my family took in a time of stress, and my sister I would die for.

If You Only Knew How God Turned My Mess Into A Message

Betrayal never wanted to care or love anyone again are better yet invest emotionally.

Angela Brock

Progression of Addiction

Now I'm out of school, welcome to adulthood. I partying, sexing, manipulation, hustling became the norm, laying up with men I didn't know better yet didn't want to know; all I saw was dollar signs and the ways to feed my addiction. Sex and drugs had become a combo meal; I couldn't have one without the other. I thought I had arrived, didn't know things were going to get worse.

Made a decision to change my environment, needed a new start, but you take things where you go. Geographic changes never help someone who is broken and needed a way to escape from heartaches—betrayal and just trying to find where your place is in life. Looking for instant gratification, I always believed in something greater than myself was protecting me from all the pain and hurt I felt inside.

As a young girl, I remember visiting different churches. I would get up every Sunday. Dress up and search for something I know today to feel the void that only God can.

Now I'm in another geographical place Rhode Island, staying with my cousin; she and her husband were stationed in the Navy. New scenery, the water surrounding the ships pulling in with Navy men, their white uniforms, and dollar signs on their heads. I was in heaven, had a candy store full of potential men to fill the void I was feeling on the inside. Meet a gentleman, he was an officer in the Navy, and I mean a gentlemen, treated me nice, took to places, but I was a scorned woman, wasn't looking for love, better yet not even knowing what love looks like.

If You Only Knew How God Turned My Mess Into A Message

This relationship went on for years, now I'm traveling to Conneticuet, to visit his family, his family and him was from

Trinidad. Their culture didn't believe in sleeping with each other before marriage, although we had already broke that tradition. So when I went to visit his family, I had to sleep with his sisters in their room, always snuck out in the middle of the night to be with him while his family was asleep.

I decided to go back home because I missed my family, still practicing those old ways of thinking. Geographical changes but never changes the person; you take you where ever you go. I'm now 20 years old, partying, sexing, drugging, but I became pregnant, with my first son Jyjuan, life was never the same, Now I'm responsible for two people, got my first place in Arlington Heights, but I always made my way back to the Hill.

Most of the time, my son Jyjuan stayed with my dad and Jan and her children, just a little girl in this big world trying to find love and acceptance in this big world. Running a little too fast at times. Now I'm in the big league, Center Avenue, the little Harlem, The Blue Room, Tim's Bar, Todd'/s Bar, Awara Club, Commerical Club, Hank and Dons, Jimmy Bar, and when I was on the east-side, I visit various clubs and bars to fill the void only God can. Drugs and I became the norm. I was always fascinated with the bad boys; the money, property, and prestige would always divert me from my primary purpose. I became a product of my environment. I had to get in where I fit in.

1987 I meet my second son's dad, thought this man had rescued me from this vicious cycled of the streets, during this relationship we conceived a baby boy 1989. In the beginning, this was the perfect relationship until crack-cocaine came into our lives; it destroyed everything that appeared to be healthy to a disaster,

Angela Brock

and it was the devil in disguise. Crack-cocaine became both of our lovers and friend.

This went on for years until God heard my cry; all I said was; *Help me*. I'm talking about a heart-felt surrender that only God can help me. The drugs were no longer able to hide the pain and suffering I had to endure. I was at the end of my rode. Life and death were around the corner. I needed to make a choice; I chose life. I didn't want to die from the disease of addiction. I finally came to the point in my life, at 29 years old, that something had to change. I got tired of the disappointment in myself and hurting the family that loved me.

If You Only Knew How God Turned My Mess Into A Message

The Beginning Of This New Way of Life Called Recover

I went into treatment this was July 25th, 1993; God gave me a second chance at life; mind you, I have already been introduced to NA through my sister Rainey; she got clean; first, I use to go to a meeting to support her, didn't know the seed was being planted through my sister, for myself. My sister's willingness and participation were watery, a new life into my spirit, and I didn't even know that even exist.

The process of discovering who I am started taking place. I know today is why it's suggested not to get into a relationship your first year in recovery, because it divert you from finding out who you are. I was in a casual fling, not with one but several young men.

One I meet in rehab, Jona, a white guy that use to make casual trips to see me in Pittsburgh; this went on for about a year until life got to hectic for him; he hung himself. I'm not going to say I was the reason for him to take his life; the disease of addiction was fully responsible. I had no feeling about it; I went on to the next available candidate, I'm not proud to say this, but it's the truth, looking for instant gratification to fill that void that only God can fill. 951 Penn Avenue is where I started talking about what was really going on. The house of pain.

I meet so many people on this particular journey, Parker, Ringo, Auto, Jamal, just a few mention that I chase my meeting like I chase the drugs. Most of us are still clean today. Through intimate ask-it basket, meeting to meetings, spriritual retreats, convention in Detroit, Starting to live convention, many NA picnics, life was looking good until reality set in dealing with me, and getting to the exact nature of why I use drugs in the beginning. 1996 November

Angela Brock

13, my sister was murder. Thank God I was building a foundation because if I haven't, I probably would have used.

Reality set in, I can no longer use unspiritual behaviors in a spiritual program undercover. I was selling drugs, and I paid the ultimate price of losing my sister. If the drugs don't kill you, the lifestyle will. I hid it well from my peers and friends in NA.

At this time, my sponsor was Bob Dimby; God rest his soul, walked me through this; depression had set in bad, I just lost my best friend, I didnt want to use, but I became obsessed with who killed her. I remember saying if I was out there in the streets, I would find out who killed her; that was a set-up for a major disaster; thank God I didn't pick-up the drug.

My sister was struggling with her sexual identity. Because I was so obsessed with her death, I found myself living her life that she hid so well, the disease is so cunning, baffleing, and powerful, it had me living my sister life style, I pick-up a female, loneiness, trying to fill a void. Still, I didnt want to use, but I needed to use something. But doing a fourth-step, it allowed me to see that I can be really comfortable living this lifestyle; it took my mother to restore me; this was Rainey's life, not yours. Wow, such a revelation.

Now I'm beginning to scratch the surface of some of my issues, like being promiscuous, looking at all the men I been with, and how I used abortions in the substitution of birth controls, 4 abortion, but only have two kids but been pregnant 6 times.

Staying in relation way past the expiration date because I didn't want to be like my mother, seeing men after men, to become her, manipulation and justification had become part of my make-up. Being with some else's man made it easy to not be emotionally available. I determine when I saw you what a sick source of reality. When I get hurt, I become vindictive and plotting, which I

If You Only Knew How God Turned My Mess Into A Message

didn't like what I was seeing, the woman in the mirror; it was time to recreate a new me; it's time to change.

For years I have been motivated and participated in my actions by fear. A scared little girl trying to find my place in the world. I knew nothing about love, intimacy, commitment, loyalty, self-respect for myself or others. I was a walking zombie, just existed physically, but emotionally, mentally, and spiritually I was broken. I started this road of recovery at Power. I stayed for eight months to build a foundation, to begin to address the rape, the abuse, and the pain I cause myself and my family, mostly my sons. Watching their mom being abuse day in and day out. My oldest suffered the most to protect his mom when I should have been protected him. Caught up in addiction where anything goes.

I was very isolated and private at this facility for women in recovery; when I went to the group, I rarely shared what was going on with me and briefly shared with my therapist due to the shame and guilt I was beginning to feel. Anger as hell, a time bomb ready to explode, I didn't want to get close to anyone because of the fear of being hurt or even being vulnerable enough to express my inner feeling. On the outside, I appeared to be a confidant, strong woman, but on the inside, I was very sensitive and shaky, and insecure, which made my recovery process harder than it should of be. I didn't know when you expose your secrets in the light of exposure, secrets die, and you can heal from the wreckage of your past.

Being at Power for eight months, I didn't reap the full benefits of becoming healthier because I had a wall so high that no one could get over it. So now I'm back in my familiar territory called home, reunited back with my kids, and my kids were acting out tremendously, but one thing I heard don't put no dope on it.

Angela Brock

My boys and I began family therapy because they're recovering from the damage I cause them. You know that the apple doesn't fall too far from the tree; they were a product of me, rebellious, confrontational, defiant, and damn right in refusal to open up. This went on into their teenage years, back and forth to Juvenile court due to unresolved issues, through my using my sons became a product of their environment. My babies were no longer participating in childlike activities. They were indulging in adult activities that put them in the hands of the criminal justice system.

The shame and guilt I felt about there situation, it was now for me to be their voice and take accountability for me introducing them to the lifestyle of hustling. I didnt know that my action would trigger down to my sons; the men I was involved with were hustlers, their mother was a hustler, even though I was clean, I still practice the lifestyle. I'm not proud of this, but it's a true story; I hustle, are dealt with hustlers to replace the things that my addiction took away from us. The bottom line consumed in fear, not being able to do for my boys. In and out of the court system with both sons into adulthood.

Through this, I became a hell-of-a advocate to find services that could help them in their mental health and criminal activities, but my sons weren't ready. It's only when the student is willing the teacher will appear. Where do I go? The street got my babies. Can you visualize handcuffs and shackles on your babies, only twelve and thirteen years old? No parent would want this for their children, but it was reality.

Thank God for a foundation because if I didn't, I probably would of use it when my sister got killed. In the reading, it says jail, institution, or death, it doesn't say what order. My sister died from a lifestyle of addiction. I lost my friend, the emptiness I felt I would not wish this on anyone. My sister was the one that planted the seed of recovery, and if I use, I would dishonor any hope that she

If You Only Knew How God Turned My Mess Into A Message

deposit in me to get this new way of living. Drug-Free and live the legacy that she didn't have the ability to live. Someone has to die for someone to live; I was chosen.

Angela Brock

Going Through a Transformation Finding My Purpose

From 1995 to 1999, I participated in a program called the Hill Collaborative for women in recovery, ran by Terri Baltimore; I went to support a friend and realize I can use the support. The intimacy we share with one another, our experiences, our strength, and our hope. We were each other support system. I finally found a place I felt connected. Being in recovery became a part of my life.

November 13,1999 Hill collaborative received a five-year grant from SAMHSA; I was chosen to be a Family Support Coordinator for the families who suffered from mental health, addiction, and their children, from the age 9-14 years of age young males. Took me right back to the community. I used drugs; you talking about a Deja VU, a blast from the past: mixed feeling, even fear. God places me there to help the people I grew up with, who head mental health, addiction. Hid it well and refuse to get services in their home.

November 13 is the day my sister was murder; that day, three years later, I become a beacon of hope to my community. This job was very challenging, but I knew it had to be a mission from God, No degree, No experience, only my own experiences, and a hope shot for families to become healthier. I had to be creative in engaging these families; the first thing I look at was their living environment, through me interacting and meeting with other Family Support Specialists from East Liberty, Wilkinsburg, Mckeesport, of course, The Hill. I got a contract with furnishing for a starter, families can get as much furniture, and our agency paid a fee of 80 dollars to fix up their home.

If You Only Knew How God Turned My Mess Into A Message

Families are now willing to allow the provider to come in a provide services. I was the in-between the families and the professional who were providing the services. Now I'm staring to see a little

Clearer. I need to help the families to get out of their comfort zones and to see how they interact with their families. Some of them have never been outside their community—program tickets for kids provided by the non-profit agency with tickets to different cultural events.

Not knowing that God was molding me into something that I didn't even know existed, a leader, with many talents, many attributes inside me. Traveling with judges, program directors, psychiatrists, a dope fen like me, sitting at the table, trying to fund a solution to get our community, our loved ones out of the vicious cycle of mental health, criminal activities. I traveled worldwide, visiting different institutions, juvinelle facilities, and being a voice for the voiceless, I never would have imagined in my entire life. I was getting paid as a consultant sharing my story, my strength, and my hope. If I knew what God was going to use me for, I probably would have messed it up.

In 1999, I meet the man I'm married to today. He came at a time when my sons were off the chain, he supported me through all their challenges, he stood in of the absence of their father, he endured many of their rebellious ways, never ran when shit got rough. He loved all of us unconditionally, I couldn't ask for a better role-model of a man to show my young cubs how to be a man, but they weren't ready. I remember my husband still today, said they're going to leave home, start their own family, make their own mistakes, but he will always be there when they're gone. Wow

Angela Brock

In the third year of the SAMHSA grant, our community based program. Community Connection for Families looked at as the model that the grant foresee it to look like. With a lot of tears, hard work, consistency, patients, determination, compassion, and most definitely God, this went on from 1999 to 2003. All the experience and knowledge I had allowed me to see what my purpose in life is supposed to be. In between these experiences, I started school for juvenile justice due to my own issues with my sons. Where I learned the language and the resources that can help me with my own dilemma. You know the saying a lot of time you can't reach your own, but you can help someone else's.

2004 God had me on another mission to help young mothers who were in the system of CYF; females are so much more challenging than males. I got hired at the Roselia Center as a counselor, through this experience I seen myself through these young women. Such anger, resentful, defiant, and rebellious. I hand my hands full. The facility reminded me of a convent that I was, that was turned into residential facilities. I began to think about the beginning of my recovery process. Power was a convent turned into a recovery house for women.

The Roselia Center's decor was all brick on the outside, in the inside old ancient windows, wood floors, a warm and serene feeling I felt. The residential place held at least 20 women and was able to go to school on site. They had a daycare inside the facility, where adopted grandmoms would care for their babies while the young women went to their appts, school, or completing their chores. It was just one big happy family.

From 2004 to 2007, I nurtured and loved on these young ladies because I didnt have and wasn't blessed to have human affection from my parents. I knew they love me through material possessions. But it's not the same to actually have someone to tell you they loved you daily; I'm proud of you, so I can remember

If You Only Knew How God Turned My Mess Into A Message

wanted attention rather it was negative are positive consequences as long as I got it. This ability didn't allow me to show affection and compassion to my sons, which I regret today. Still, I also have had the opportunity to break this family cycle through recovery.

These young ladies help me get in touch with the inner child in me, the one who has been hurt, who has been violated of their innocents; I was starting to heal through helping them heal. After working for a year at Roselia, I was offered a superior position due to my determination and loyalty, and consistency to the ladies; they look at me as a positive role-model for their agency.

While working ay Roselia, my mother's illness turn for worst; she had Stage 4 Lung Cancer; I needed to make a choice to be there for my mom are my job, I choose to be there for my mom. The labor of love came in its right season. It was time to do some big girl stuff, make a sacrifice for someone else other than me. I remember like it was yesterday when I got the call from my mom's doctor that's she's going to possibly or eventually die. The woman who gave me life is slowly dying, and I had to witness her suffering for two years and couldn't put no dope on the feeling. You talking about being powerless.

At this time, my grandson was in the system, his dad was again incarcerated, and my husband was going through his own problems. I felt so alone, didn't know if I was coming are going, I was on auto-pilot. I began to look for programs to assist my mom, so she can stay home. At this time, my mom and grandmother have moved to Presley High Rise on the North Side, so they both can be in the same building to look after one another. Life in Pittsburgh was a blessing; I work under them to keep my mom in her home; they called it a consumer model, which means a family member can work for the consumer.

Angela Brock

A couple of years went by, my mom's situation wasn't improving; she was making constant trips back and forth to the hospital, her cancer worsens, where treatment was no longer an option. Now we were faced with a decision to just keep her comfortable. Every day I would visit the hospital and nursing home to visit my mom, never went at the same time to keep the staff on their feet to care for my mother. September 29, 2009, the angel of death call my mom home.

Life was never the same. My mom was the rock of the family, but it's something about God. He allowed me to grieve while she was living and gave me the opportunity for closure and most definitely peace and acceptance with the situation. When you love someone so much, you don't want to watch them suffer; many nights, on my watch, she was in so much pain. My prayers change to God; if she's not going to get better, take her. I'm talking about a deeper level of surrender. That woman has persevered through many obstacles. I thought the woman had nine lives. When the doctors said on numerous occasions to get her personal stuff in order. God said I show yah whos, God.

I remember the day the doctor said there's nothing else they can do, that day I watch the fight to live to leave my mom, she was always a fighter, but that day she no longer wanted to fight anymore, she was tired, and she made peace and acceptance with God. It was 3:45 am I received the call my mom had pass. I knew she had died like I knew my sister had died; there was something about the spirit being connected to someone you feel them. Feeling like some left you. I really can't explain the feeling, a sense of emptiness.

My mom's death impacted our family; she was the string that kept us connected; when that string was cut, so was the rest of the family. I tried hard to keep our family together, but everybody was doing their own thing. It's crazy when one life can keep people

If You Only Knew How God Turned My Mess Into A Message

together, and when that life is no longer present, neither is the connection.

Time went on, I was enrolled in CCAC for criminal justice and DA counseling, been trying to complete this for years, but my home life was in trouble, so I had to put school on the back burner, my sons were off the chain, and I couldn't focus on my own personal goals. Going in and out of the Juvenile Justice system, both of my sons and I became damn good at advocating for them to get the proper treatment. At one point in time, both of the sons were on house arrest. I felt like I was being penalized. 2012 I finally got my diploma for certification and two credits away from my Associates in Criminal Justice. This was May 17th, 2012. Three months later, my Dad got sick, Diagnosis with 4th stage Liver Cancer, this was on the first of July, and on July 17th, he passed in 2012.

I was devasted this is one death God didn't prepare me for. I was just beginning to develop a father and daughter relationship. He was just at my graduation, and now he's gone. Both of my sons and my husband were facing some serious criminal charges and were waiting to go to trial. I know they say God doesn't give you know more than you can handle, but damn, my recovery was being tested. My husband was innocent in all this but was pulled into my sons' mess because he was connected to them. I couldn't allow the Justice system to use my husband as the fall guy to turn evidence on my sons. I got my husband a lawyer; thank God my dad left me money for just that. My husband and my youngest son got off, but my oldest son was sentenced and did time until 2014.

During the funeral, I remember feeling like an outcast; my father had raised another family. Only through recovery I was able to maintain my sanity and my cool and do what was asked of me by

Angela Brock

my dad. The feeling of loneliness, not being apart, was so embittered so deep in my spirit. There was an mgt across the street from Jones's funeral, the Red Door, that's where I found myself going, while my extended family was out in the parking lot fighting and my sons were also involved. It was crazy, but it was also a blessing I wasn't apart of the insanity. Right then, I decided I didn't no longer have to be apart of a family that really didn't care for me anyway. When my dad died, the memories of them did too.

I no longer had to share my dad; he was gone, but I insisted that my sons stayed connected because they loved my sons and they were good to them. Visiting wasn't the same without my dad's present. My dad was the light that shines on that household; when he died, so did the light over that house. It was filled with evil, hatred, jealousy, envy, and I no longer wanted to be apart of it. Everybody crying victim, everybody having a sense of entitlement, my job was done honoring my dad's wishes.

Right after my father's passing, I felt the need to be connected to women, to uplift me, support me, encourage me, shine love over me, and it wasn't happening in Pittsburgh. Not even the women in recovery. During my internship, I was introduced to a bunch of women from all walks of life from Atlanta who had a traveling agency, the best decision I ever made. I began traveling all over the world with these ladies, Puerto Rico, Saint Thomas, St Martin, Barbados, where I start reading and sharing my poetry. My father's death forced me to write because the pain was so real. Many other places I traveled, and every time I traveled, I took a piece of my mom.

Spreading her ashes on whatever island I visit. It was a spiritual experience. I began to start healing with the help of these women. I finally found some women I connected with; it was like a sisterhood. I was searching for in my own city but never was able to get even in recovery. There were a few women I connected

If You Only Knew How God Turned My Mess Into A Message

with. I was never the one who needed to be socially accepted by others or needed to be surrounded by a lot of people to feel a sense of security are validation. I fought hard not to lose me to be with you. I didn't get clean to lose myself. I'm in a program to find myself. So this process has been a lonely road but rewarding because I'm now comfortable in my own skin.

2015 My buddy, my friend, my shopping buddy, my listening ear, had made a decision to take her life; this was December 26, 2014, on her birthday, I kind of knew she was depressed, but the severity I didn't know. I spoke with her that morning, she sounds like she was under the weather, to wish her a happy birthday. Thinking back, the last couple of times together, she didn't seem like herself. It was like his body was there, but her mind was somewhere else, like an out-of-body experience. She wasn't such a big talker; my friend talk in riddles; you had to read between the line to figure out what she was saying.

I believe she was trying to tell me something, but she was so caught up in depression, and especially she came from an era that what was done and said in the house stayed in the house. I remember one day she came out and said she got to go to Hillman Cancer Center, and I asked, "Do you have cancer? She never responded. After her suicide, this is when Macy's was open, and the sales associates told me my friend had cancer, I blame myself for not probing for answers, not that I could have made her change her decision, but I could have supported her through whatever she was going through. Shopping has never been the same. We would leave out early in the morning until the evening.

My friend was a classy lady, a lovable person, and there's not a minute I don't think about her. I was looking at my wedding

Angela Brock

picture, she was my maid of honor, such a beautiful spirit always supported me in anything I did. I love receiving gifts from her; very unique and had so many sentimental values. I miss you, Lady I hope you found some peace; you no longer have to fight the enemy within.

If You Only Knew How God Turned My Mess Into A Message

New Beginning

Janurary 25, 2015, exactly one month after my friend's suicide, I was offered a partial scholarship to attend Geneva College Adult Learning Program. I had received these offers before but ignored the invitation until my friend took her life, something inside of me can't believe she's gone. I started my Bachelor's in Community Ministry and Leadership. I start learning what God will is for me. Through the classes I took, my faith had grown because all our assignment had to have a biblical approach but using our personal experience.

Talking about feelings, some fear, not feeling like I can measure up with my peers, always felt inadequate, but I persevered through it all. I showed up when I didn't even want to be there. God was shifting and stretching me, and I was developing more spiritual enlightenment. Through attending this 18-month program, I gain so much insight spiritually about myself. I attended from 2015 to 2017 which I gain my degree in Community Ministry and leadership.

Angela Brock

Things Are Getting Real, Death All Around Me

In 2017 I got a call from my step-son's mother to let me know that DJ had got shot and killed; my heart felt so heavy, I was in urgent care and had walking Pneumonia, and all I could do is cry and try to get myself together to tell my husband. That was one of the saddest memories I could ever imagine. DJ age 28, my son Jy was in a serious car accident the same day. God spared my son and took mines DJ who was like my son. I couldn't imagine how she felt, but I need to be supportive because we both love DJ. 2018 my other son I raised at the age of 34 didn't want to stop drinking and had a massive heart attack. He had lost the will to live; such a young life couldn't find anything in life was worth living,

RIP Lil Rome; this was in February 2018, from Mom Duke. That's what he called me. July 25th, my clean date, my grandfather died. I had the opportunity to return the favor that my grandfather gave me; he believed in me when I didn't believe in myself. Took me to treatment; at this time, I had just celebrated 25years clean when God called him home. Through recovery, I was able to walk with God, make the funeral arrangements, and hold my head up with integrity, unconditional love, even though that last day I had to walk it alone.

On August 22, 2018, my birthday, My firstborn, Jyjuan had to face his demons; his fate was in the hands of the law, which was the last time I physically was able to hug my child. It was a long walk to the courthouse; we had an in-depth discussion about getting his life together and dealing with the issues that keeps him going back and forth to jail.

It's crazy we had the same color coordination; I had on a fuchsia-colored jumpsuit, and my son had on a fuchsia pink polo-shirt,

If You Only Knew How God Turned My Mess Into A Message

with some Khaki polo pants; he gave me numbers and money he had saved for worse case outcomes. He knew he was going to jail, and he was tired of running from himself. In my heart, I knew too.

After court, that was the longest walk again alone; it was my birthday; I will never forget that day in my entire life. You talking about a hole in your soul, and you couldn't do anything to fix it, powerless; that's when I had no choice to turn my son's life under the care of God. I'm talking about when you're connected to a spirit; my youngest son Jaylon felt his mom's pain, pick me up from the court, made sure his mom had a nice birthday. My sons were raised to be each other's brothers keepers. That day one couldn't make sure their mom had a nice birthday; the other stood in a position to be his mother keeper. It's always been me and boys against the world; we got to have each other's back because all we have is each other.

Every situation we experience, rather it's your own, and someone you love goes through, God has his hands in it, might not see it right away, God was working it out. My son's situation allow me to tap in some giving gift.

Love was a motivator, compassion was my initiator to help moms like myself to navigate through the criminal justice system. A friend sent me an article of a powerful organization Heinz Endowment, a woman Carmen Anderson wrote November 29, 2017, happen to be my son's Jyjuans birthday. The woman was talking all about the needs in our community and the jails, the same stuff my son was talking about that is needed, and he had a vision of a program that would be effective in jail and once they are released. I sent him the article, my son wrote her.

It was 10pm, I took a shower, I pray, and proceeding to email the Director of Equality and Social justice to see if she received my

Angela Brock

son's letter. 10:30pm I received a call from her secretary that Mrs. Anderson wanted to meet Jyjuan Brocks mother, who wrote her the letter. Marcus Harvey and I went to Heinz Endowment for the conference call; she was so impressed with his letter that she wanted to start groups with mothers whose child was incarcerated how we can start addressing change, give hope, and assistance.

I was responsible for getting the ladies together, and Mrs. Anderson and the staff facilitates it. I wanted to have a diverse group that consists of mothers, professional law enforcement, clinical background, probation officers, housing assistance, aftercare during and after release. It was a very intense discussion group, with providers who already assisting inmates with family reunification, probation reform; our meetings went on monthly for eight months.

Now we're at the place in this process to get a name for the group MOMS; Mothers On The Move. Advocacy programs assist families with support, referrals, and resources to advocate and navigate through the ciminal justice system for their loved ones. Because of my sons' vision and situation, the ladies and I began to develop this support system.

I realized everything in life is for a reason; in the beginning, we look at it as a bad thing, but it was a blessing in reality. My son was not arrested; he was rescued; God saves him from himself. My son, JyJuan is now an author of two books, and he is mentually and emotionally more stable than he has ever been. A lot of the time he's the teacher, and I'm the student. He always stresses to me; physically, he's confined, but mentally and emotionally, he's free.

Through editing my son's book and having his voice be heard, I was motivated through his influence to come to my truth. The

If You Only Knew How God Turned My Mess Into A Message

Pandemic also had a big part; to go inside of myself and heal from

all the things that were intended to destroy me, but all it did is made me stronger. Being transparent is not an easy thing to do; I no longer got to hide behind phony images of myself to be socially accepted by man but by God. If you only Knew how God turned my mess into a message.

Angela Brock

Recovery Poem

Recovery is like being in the wilderness, then you start finding out things about yourself. When I began to sort through the contradiction and confusion of my life, then and only then I began to get a better perspective of my life. Drugs became my lover and friend; I never knew how my days were going to end. Running from city to city, belittling myself for some cash. Just a little girl in this big world, trying to find love and acceptance from anyone that crosses my path.

Addiction robbed me like a thief in the night; most of the time, I didn't know if it was day are night. Matter of fact didn't know how my days were going to end. All I knew is that I had to get it in. The drugs where a temporary relief to cover up all the shame and guilt, and I was too embarrassed to express to anyone how I felt. Momma wasn't there to protect me from the disease; she was so caught up in her own thing. Daddy was also running the street; he was caught up in the same disease that imprisoned me.

Identity being sold didn't know how powerful disease had a hold. The disease of addiction is cunning, baffling, and powerful, had the power and positive choices; I once had dreams and hopes but the dope control any hope. Lost site of life, At one time, had a clear path of insight. Easy come- easy go, I'm now at the end of my road. Now I'm clean from what the disease has done to me. God isn't finished with me yet. He cleaned me up, dust me off, stood me up to give back what was freely given to me.

Now I'm free from what the disease has done to me; I can't wait to see what He will do next; my chapters in my life are not over yet, still work to be done. God is the architect of my life, the Holy-

If You Only Knew How God Turned My Mess Into A Message

Spirit is my provider, The people in NA are my support system. I've been

blessed to be placed in a room full of people that drugs was their major problem, Koryn Hawthorne, famous music gospel singer, sang, *Aint nobody stopping my shine, because I got Jesus on my side, what the enemy planned for my down-fall, turned out to be the greatest victory of my life.*

When life comes at you fast and hard, all you want to do is make things right. Won't he do it? He said he will fight your battle when you have a sleepless night. God hand-pick me from what the disease has done to me. To tell my story, If you only knew how God turned my mess into a message.

Angela Brock

End with This

We live in a world and, combined with different cultures, think happiness is defined on what we had. Yes, money, property, and prestige can be a temporary solution to the void we have inside of us. Instant gratification is just a temporary solution. Happiness is something that you feel about yourself; nothing can replace it.

The hardest war to win is the one you don't realize your fighting, and the hardest enemy to defeat is the one you don't even know exist. (Mathew Kelly). There are four words that are challenging when you are trying to seek a spiritual life; we find it in the fifth line, Our Father, Thy will be done, that's telling me that you can come willingly to Gods will are with a fight, but His will is going to be done.

We resist things for all sorts of reasons, especially finding happiness, watching others' lives with family, friends, colleagues, and thinking we can mimic their lives instead of finding happiness in our own lives.

Then you start watching similar patterns of laziness, procrastination cripple people personally and professionally. I'm guilty of this. I am always sabotaging my chances of success and happiness repeatedly, but that's not where happiness starts first, it starts with you, finding your purpose, worth, value, and most definitely your truth. Stop resisting happiness. It's around the corner. As we go into the New Year it's important to let go of any baggage that's holding you down that doesnt allow us to live our best life.

God Bless You All

If You Only Knew How God Turned My Mess Into A Message

www.ingramcontent.com/pod-product-compliance
Lightning Source LLC
Chambersburg PA
CBHW071145090426
42736CB00012B/2242